An Insider's Experience of
Insurgency in India's North-East

Anthem South Asian Studies
Series Editor: Crispin Bates

Other titles in the series:

Brosius, Christiane *Empowering Visions* (2005)
Mills, Jim (ed) *Sport in South Asia* (2005)
Joshi, Chitra *Lost Worlds: Indian Labour and its Forgotten Histories* (2005)
Dasgupta, Biplab, *European Trade and Colonial Conquest* (2005)
Kaur, Raminder *Performative Politics and the Cultures of Hinduism* (2005)
Rosenstein, Lucy *New Poetry in Hindi* (2004)
Shah, Ghanshyam, *Caste and Democratic Politics in India* (2004)
Van Schendel, Willem *The Bengal Borderland: Beyond State and Nation in South Asia* (2004)

# An Insider's Experience of Insurgency in India's North-East

*By*
LT GENERAL J R MUKHERJEE, PVSM, AVSM, VSM (Retd)

Anthem Press

Anthem Press
An imprint of Wimbledon Publishing Company
75-76 Blackfriars Road, London SE1 8HA
www.anthempress.com

This edition first published by Anthem Press 2005

Copyright © Lt General J R Mukherjee PVSM, AVSM, VSM (Retd) 2005

The moral right of the authors has been asserted.
All rights reserved. Without limiting the rights under copyright reserved above, no part of this publication may be reproduced, stored or introduced into a retrieval system, or transmitted, in any form or by any means (electronic, mechanical, photocopying, recording or otherwise), without the prior written permission of both the copyright owner and the above publisher of this book.

*British Library Cataloguing in Publication Data*
A catalogue record for this book is available from the British Library.

*Library of Congress Cataloguing in Publication Data*
A catalogue record for this book has been requested.

1 3 5 7 9 10 8 6 4 2

ISBN 1 84331 700 1 (HB)

Cover illustration: Chabi Datt

Printed in India

# An Insider's Experience of Insurgency in India's North-East

## Lt General J R Mukherjee, PVSM, AVSM, VSM (Retd)

An alumni from National Defence Academy, the Indian Military Academy and the National Defence College, Lt General J R Mukherjee, PVSM, AVSM, VSM (Retd) was commissioned into the Assam Regiment (Infantry) of The Indian Army in 1964 and retired in 2005 as Chief of Staff, Eastern Command, Indian Army.

Professionally attended Staff College at Camberley in the UK and the Senior and Higher Air Command Courses of the Indian Army, Lt General J R Mukherjee, PVSM, AVSM, VSM (Retd) served for over 41 years in the Indian Army on active, wartime and operational command – out of which he spent more than 23 years in the north eastern region handling diverse assignments.

In 1999, Lt General J R Mukherjee, PVSM, AVSM, VSM (Retd) became the Chief of Staff of the corps stationed for operations in Kashmir when the Pakistani conflict at Kargil. He then commanded the same corps in Kashmir and was acclaimed for his contribution towards restoring internal security at the hour of crises. He has also been awarded the Param Vishisht Seva Medal (PVSM), the Vishisht Seva Medal (VSM) and the Ati Vishisht Seva Medal (AVSM) for his rich contribution to the Indian Army and for his efforts towards bringing insurgency under control in the northeast.

Lt General J R Mukherjee, PVSM, AVSM, VSM (Retd) has plans to make use of his leisure time by way of sharing his many untold stories.

Lt Gen S.K. Pillai, PVSM (Retd.)

'Vichitra', Jawahar Nagar
Trivandrum - 695 003
Tel : 0471-2724935
e-mail : sushil@md5.vsnl.net.in

# FOREWORD

The title of this remarkable book says it all. Lt General J R Mukherjee, PVSM, AVSM, VSM (Retd) is an 'insider' with over twenty four years of service in our north-eastern region in various capacities ranging from a company commander to Chief of Staff, Eastern Command. In addition, he has an insider's Regimental and familial ties with the north-east. Added to this is his considerable experience in tackling insurgencies not only in our north-eastern states but also as a Corps Commander in J&K during the Kargil War. His views and recommendations, many of which are radical and thought provoking will, I am sure, bring in a freshness to what has unfortunately become a stale and repetitive discourse on the insurgencies in our north eastern states.

This book, notable for its brevity and focus on essentials, can be read at various levels. It could be a reading as an introductory book for those interested in or posted to the north-east; an aide in understanding the complex problems of each of the eight north eastern states and North Bengal; a catalyst for new initiatives and for prompting re-examination and debate on north eastern policies; and finally as a case study of how well intentioned but flawed policies generate violence.

Three points which specially stand out in this book are the need for applying a deep historical, geographical and socio-economic perspective to the search for solutions to the insurgencies in the north eastern states. Secondly, the need for a holistic approach when evolving conflict resolution measures and thirdly the need for full utilisation of human resources in ensuring the aims of National Security which are to ensure the freedom, well being and safety of our citizens and protection of our core values and interests.

The author rightly points out that insurgencies and ethnic conflicts in the north east have a long history going back well before the 12th and 13th Centuries. The usual time line of dating the commencement of insurgencies post-1947 is wrong and leads to incorrect conclusions.

The need for a holistic approach, is illustrated by showing how foreign policy is generally not taken into account when considering the insurgencies in our eastern border lands, and if at all it is, the discourse restricts itself to denial of insurgent bases and conduct of joint operations with our neighbouring countries. The author suggests a far wider holistic scope in our foreign policy that includes cooperation in a whole gamut of measures including joint operations in checking illegal finance, weapons, fissile materials and drug flows as well as intelligence sharing mechanisms in so far as tackling insurgency and terrorism is concerned. Above all, one of the aims of our foreign policy should be to convince friendly nations that our security is vital to their own interests as is perceived by them in regard to Saudi Arabia (Oil), Pakistan (ally in the Great Game and in the fight against terrorism) and Japan (bulwark in East Asia). Unfortunately, this degree of integration of security concerns with foreign policy has yet to be attained.

Thirdly, the full capability of human resources has yet to be utilised. For the first time, a detailed recommendation has been made urging the utilisation of serving and ex-servicemen in the development of the region. The human aspect of insurgencies is dealt with by policy makers in a pedestrian manner and is an area for reform. The state of our uncoordinated efforts to win the hearts and minds of the people is appalling with each Ministry concerned, working out schemes on their own. The existing mechanisms to integrate the people of the north-east with the rest of the country are inadequate, as has been empirically proved. A lack of understanding and empathy for the unique psyche of each of our north-eastern tribes continues, despite the passage of almost six decades since Independence.

One of the disturbing aspects of our policies on the north eastern region is the lack of fresh ideas on how to tackle what is a fast changing, dynamic situation there. Much of the discourse still concerns old, outdated concepts such as 'no development before peace'; 'political solution instead of a military solution', and the choice of a 'strategy of attrition to wear down the insurgents'. The fond belief that an agreement with the leaders of the 'mother of insurgencies' – the NSCN (I-M) will bring peace to the entire north-east is fallacious. Indeed, we need to look beyond Accords in working out future contingencies.

A newspaper report of August 18, 1995, gives details of a three-pronged strategy for the development of the north-east. I find the same strategy being presented afresh at a recent conclave of Chief Ministers of insurgency-ridden states. There is a sense of *déjà vu* on reading a news item of October 15, 2004 on the 18th Annual Conference of DGPs and IGPs of the north eastern states, wherein a Special Director, Intelligence Bureau 'stressed the need for setting up a mechanism for regular coordination between the police forces in the region and the Security and Central Para-Military Forces'. The same recommendation has been regularly made during the last five decades of internal security in the north-eastern region!

The need to come up with a fresh approach to meet the changed external and internal security environment is all too evident as is the resistance to change by stake-holders for maintaining the status quo. This book offers a number of fresh suggestions such as consociation politics, state boundaries to be considered mainly for administrative purposes, increased economic inter-action and a quickened pace of modernisation, particularly in information technology; improved surface and air communications; development and skilling of local entrepreneurs and focusing on preparing for the future when the Asian Highway brings with it a host of benefits and negative influences; and doing away with Inner Line restrictions while allaying tribal fears of being swamped by outsiders. The book avoids the earlier security paradigm of emphasis on military operations, though this aspect is given its due importance.

This book is an important addition to the literature on insurgencies in our north-eastern states. It is both informant and catalyst and takes a contemporary view of the dynamic and changing nature of the insurgencies that ill serve the people of the north-east. The essence of the book is clear – we need to evolve fresh counter-insurgency, growth and development strategies and shed those that are no longer relevant. Lt General J R Mukherjee PVSM, AVSM, VSM (Retd) has suggested a way out. It is for these reasons that his book must be read.

# CONTENTS

Preface     xiii

## SECTION I: ISSUES AND PROBLEMS OF INSURGENCY, GROWTH AND DEVELOPMENT

1. Effects of Geography and History     3
2. Assam     17
3. Nagaland     27
4. Manipur     39
5. Meghalaya, Mizoram and Tripura     47
6. Arunachal, Sikkim and North Bengal     55
7. Role of Servicemen/Ex-servicemen     65
8. India's Foreign Relations, the Effects of Geo-power Politics and Events in Neighbouring Countries     73

## SECTION II: RESOLUTION

9. Foreign policy with Reference to the North-East     87
10. Internal Policy     93
11. Economic Aspects     99
12. Politico – Military Policy     105
13. Conclusion: Problem Resolution for the North-East     117

List of Abbreviations     131

Selected Bibliography     133

Index     139

# PREFACE

India's north-east has been beset by problems arising from lack of economic development and insurgency for long. Though the reasons for these are manifold, they primarily lie within the region's sociological, geographic, historical, economic and political spheres. This book is aimed at giving the reader an overview of the major crises that hamper advancement in the north-east, with the hope that it would assist in arriving at solutions.

The 'north-east' comprises the states of Assam, Arunachal, Nagaland, Mizoram, Manipur, Tripura, Meghalaya, Sikkim, and North Bengal, which though hasn't yet been officially included in the region, forms an integral part of it. The north-east is an area clouded with lack of knowledge and ambiguity for most of our citizens. That it is today an underdeveloped area, troubled with strife, insurgency and low-intensity conflict with our neighbours, where modernity is in conflict with tradition, is largely due to the indifference of the rest of the country. With over 500 different ethnic groups, of which 110 are major, and a consequent diverse ethnic sub-nationalism governed by the primordial values of 'tribe – land – autonomy', there is only one commonality – a partially mongoloid heritage. People are in conflict with the state and other ethnic groups, because they feel their values have not been respected and they have been alienated by segregation, social deprivation, lack of development, exploitation because they look, speak and believe differently. There is a sense prevailing within the region that governing authorities have persistently failed to make efforts to understand and resolve, a problem which is compounded by the constant erosion of people through increasing immigration into other states.

I write this book, as like many of us, I feel agitated at the way in which those in authority handle the north-east. Over 41 years ago, I was commissioned into the ASSAM Regiment, whose recruitment is from the entire north-east, and have ever since been in close touch with the men of my regiment, the ex-servicemen and their families. I have served for twenty-four years all over the north-east in a wide variety of appointments, and have had extensive contact with the people; I have, as a result of my close association, developed a great deal of love for the region's people. One of my aims in writing this book is therefore to put across the frank views and acute dissatisfaction that most of the people of the north-east, including many bureaucrats, government and police officials, politicians, intellectuals and technocrats feel, but do not have the energy or will to express. Further, with government servants literally being muzzled over by the expression of opinions or dissent with government policy, I consider it my sacred duty within the bounds of the 'official' norms, to put across the difficulties people have faced and continue to face while trying to eke out a living in the north-east. I hope that this book would be read by some of those in authority and that it would contribute to a more rational and humane handling of the situation.

I also owe the writing of this book to my 'Comrades in Arms' in the Indian Army, who are unable to publicly voice their concerns over faulty policies that are sometimes put into play. I owe it to them to verbalise the concerns I have had while in service that were voiced officially but not heard.

I also write this book with the hope that it would be read by all those who have to serve and function in the north-east – particularly government servants, police/CPO/PMF officials, army officers, intellectuals and businessmen. People invariably go to the north-east only for short tenures or periods. I therefore hope that this book would educate them and assist them in more efficient functioning. I feel this is important as this book is based on a wealth and lifetime of experience – not only my own, but also that of my comrades, all my friends in all the other walks of life and those on the other side of the fence including the insurgents with whom I have interacted at length.

I have risen to a high rank in the Army and held many important appointments only thanks only to the devotion, love, respect and sincere endeavours of these wonderful people – I therefore will always be indebted to them. This book is dedicated to these brave men and their families.

I must also express my sincere thanks and gratitude to my wife Linda, also a north-easterner; my daughter Chabi who designed the cover of this book; Lt Gen S K Pillai, PVSM, (Retd), a close friend and guide,

# PREFACE

in my view one of the greatest authorities on the north-east and who has been kind enough to write a 'Foreword' to this Book; Mr Sanjoy Hazarika, a renowned journalist and authority on the north-east, whose views I greatly respect; General Shanker Roychoudhury, PVSM, ex Chief of Army Staff, (Retd), who has given me tremendous support and a write up for this book, friends and colleagues; my publisher Wimbledon Publishing Company Limited, UK; and my editor Arundhati Nath, who have all given me their wholehearted and overwhelming support and views in the writing and publication of this book.

I have written this book more from the point of view of a social scientist than as a soldier as I am strongly of the view that most of the concerns stem from social, economic and political factors. Many are rooted in the history and the geography of the region.

I have organised this book into 13 chapters. The first chapter gives a geographical and historical overview and a perspective of the problems caused by these parameters. I have thereafter given an overview of each north-eastern state and its major crises. My suggestions at resolution of problems of all these states, dictated by my research and experience of the region, have been dealt with together in separate chapters as the destinies and ills of all these states are closely interlinked. The possibilities of solutions lie within the realms of foreign, internal and economic policies and finally a well-framed politico–military policy.

A large amount of the material given in this book has no reference material as it is gleaned from contacts with a huge number of people from all walks of life, my prolonged stay in the region, which has shaped my personal experiences and perceptions. I have however over the past many years read on the subject extensively – books, media reports and articles, journals, assessments, official unclassified releases and reports and the storehouse of material available on the Internet. All this information has been interwoven into the fabric of this book. I have not put down any footnotes giving detailed referencing, as is the usual norm in such books. I have however added a bibliography with details of the relatively recent material I have sourced, and I must acknowledge to the authors of this material that it has been of great help to me.

I have in this book made certain categorical statements – including naming countries and blaming them for adding to our country's woes by waging a proxy war against us. Adequate proof is available in official releases, media, circumstantial evidence and even foreign reports on the subject. I have mentioned a few of these in the bibliography. I must also state that a lot of the material, particularly the later half, is one of perceptions based on circumstantial evidence, which has been given in the subject matter – obviously I remain culpable for expressing the same.

I do not by any means claim to be the gospel in terms of possible solutions. I have merely given certain options with the hope that these would at least prompt re-examination of policy by those in authority and provide healthy debate and food for thought on a somewhat neglected subject.

I must at the outset apologise to those who feel aggrieved at any of the views expressed in this book. The views are totally my own and are based on perceptions which have been shaped over a long period of time. I have tried my best to put across unbiased and rational ideas in the best interests of the people of the north-east and the nation – these views may not be in tune with everyone's – but they are directed at the larger issue of finding answers to the problems which have plagued us for long.

# Section I
# ISSUES AND PROBLEMS OF INSURGENCY, GROWTH AND DEVELOPMENT

# 1
# EFFECTS OF GEOGRAPHY AND HISTORY

The geography and history of a region naturally shape the contours of its people, their ethnic groupings, culture, traditions, value system and way of life. They also indicate the patterns of migration of ethnic groups and reasons for the same. In a nutshell, as would be seen from the forthcoming analysis, it is a region's geography and history that largely contribute to the problems and prospects of its people and their destiny.

**The Lie of the Land**
Geographically, the north-east consists of the states of Assam, Nagaland, Manipur, Mizoram, Tripura, Arunachal, Sikkim and though not officially accepted yet as part of it – North Bengal. It is definitely an integral part of the region covering an area of about 300,000 sq km, with a population of about 46 million. The north-east is connected to the rest of India over a narrow stretch of plains through North Bengal and Assam known as the Siliguri Corridor (also called the Chicken's Neck by some), which leads into the Brahmaputra river valley plains. The Brahmaputra valley plains are about 70 to 90 km wide and 900 km long. West of Guwahati the valley widens substantially to merge with Bangladesh and the Gangetic plains.

The Himalayan mountains of Nepal, Sikkim, North Bengal, Bhutan, Arunachal and Tibet bound the Brahmaputra and the Gangetic valley plains to the north, the eastern hills link India and Myanmar to the east, and the Meghalaya-Karbi Anglong plateau, the Barak River valley and the plains of Bangladesh to the south. The Cachar and North Cachar hills, the Manipur valley, the Mizoram and Manipur hill ranges and the piedmont plains of Tripura in turn bound the Barak valley. The entire hill and mountain sector forming 70% of the region is generally covered with forests and is dissected by a large number of major rivers with deep gorges flowing into the main river systems. These rivers are surrounded by high mountain ranges, which effectively segregate the valleys making them mutually distinct. Migration routes have therefore also followed these valleys, as it is these that have offered access. The entire hill sector is also heavily forested thereby increasing its inaccessibility to the extent that ethnic groups have therefore lived in near total isolation from each other.

Consequently, population groups residing in each of these valleys have retained their exclusive identity and from where their primordial value systems of 'tribe – land – autonomy' have taken root. Geography has therefore dictated the distinctiveness of the inhabitants; the region's topography has caused high population densities and created key accesses to the hill areas through the main river valleys. Thus the Siliguri Corridor and the Brahmaputra valley, which are the main population centres and communication hubs, form the core while the hill sectors form the fringe regions. The valleys with their rich fertile soil, abundant natural resources which include fifty per cent of India's tea, twenty per cent of its oil, huge forest wealth and large coal and mineral reserves; varied climatic conditions extending from tropical to alpine (based on location and altitude, varying from 600–18000 feet) and tremendous scenic beauty, have throughout history been a source of attraction for migrating and invading hordes through the mountain passes and the river valleys. The constant migration ensured a melting pot of various cultures and ethnic groups and shaped a rich and colourful historical past. The region also has a marked individuality being a transitional area between high Asia, Indo-China and the Gangetic – Brahmaputra plains – it consequently has a multitude of ethnic groups with predominantly mongoloid traits. The gateways to the region have traditionally been across the mountain passes of the Himalaya and the eastern hills as also through the Siliguri Corridor, Cachar and Tripura.

## History

A study of history of the region is important as its analysis highlights the multitude of resident ethnic groups, characteristics and value systems which mould their views and give rise to social, economic and political issues which are important to them. Understanding these issues is crucial to putting the region's problems in perspective and thereby inching towards resolving them.

An analysis of the history of the north-east is indicative, to a large extent, of perpetual migrations into the region, perhaps due to its being a land of plenty with a salubrious climate and sparse population The types of ethnic migrations can be categorised broadly into mongoloid groups from Greater Tibet, Mongolia and China, ethnic groups from Myanmar and erstwhile Indo-China; Mon Khmer groups; Aryans, Negritos and Dravidians from the West; Muslims through Bengal; Gurkhas from Nepal; Marwari businessmen from Rajasthan in fairly large numbers; Adivasi labour for tea plantations; Bihari and other labourers from central India and Bihar; and Bengalis in recent times.

## Earliest Inhabitants: Negritos, Austrics, Bodos, Nagas and Arunachali Tribes

North-eastern history, particularly the ancient history is to a large extent not properly documented, with the sources broadly being:

- Archaeology – neoliths, epigraphs, numismatics
- Anthropology
- Texts – Vedic and classical literature – the Puranas, Tantrik, Budhist and Assamese literature – the Ahom Chronicles (*Buranjis*), other historical works, foreign accounts, government studies and other records;
- Folklore that has been handed down from generation to generation.

These indicate the earliest inhabitants to be of Austric stock (Mon Khmer akin to the Munds in Bihar, also similar to the Papuans and Andamanese), now residing primarily in Meghalaya (Khasis and Jaintias) and Karbi Anglong (Karbis, earlier called Mikirs in Assam) and a limited Dravidian and Negrito presence which has today been almost totally merged with the Tibeto – Burmans and Austrics or annhilated. A few thousand years BC onwards, there were waves of Mongoloid migrations – different tribes and clans – (Tibeto – Burmans of Indo-Chinese stock) including the Bodo group of tribes whose original abode is believed to have been Mongolia, Greater Tibet and north-west China, who occupied and established control over the entire area from Uttar Pradesh eastwards, after pushing the Austrics/ Dravidians/Negritos into remote areas, well before the Aryan migrations. They were called the Kiratas and Mlechas, reference to which can be found in the great Indian epics. The descendants of these tribes are found in Nepal, Sikkim (Lepchas), North Bengal

(Kamtapuris) (Koch), Assam (Bodo-Kachari-Dimasa-Chutiya-Marans-Rajbanshis and some other tribes), Garo Hills (Garos of Meghalaya), Meitei tribes of Manipur, Tripuris of Tripura, Bhutan (originally inhabited by Austrics and then the Bodo groups till overwhelmed by the Tibetans), the many tribes of Arunachal including the Akas, Adis, Mishmis, and the present day Naga tribes. These tribes managed to hold their own identity for a long period of time.

Different groups migrating from slightly different areas and in a different time span are in many cases today treated as separate ethnic groups on account of dialect/language differences though in reality they may well be of the same broad origin. These mongoloid migrations have continued through the entire period of our known history and in fact continue even now.

During the period before the Aryan migrations, legends and the epics indicate that the Bodos had established a great kingdom which survived for many generations, called Kamrupa, with the capital at Pragjyotishpura (Guwahati) extending over Bihar, Bengal, Orissa, the entire Assam plains and some of the hill areas of the north-east.

**The Aryans**

The Aryan migrations that originated from Central Asia, after taking control of north India, spilled further east around the period of the birth of Christ onwards and progressively overwhelmed the Austric, Negrito and Mongoloid ethnic groups in Uttar Pradesh, Bihar, Bengal and Orissa. Aryan migrations into the eastern part of North Bengal and lower (western) Assam plains ultimately led to the adoption of Vedic and Hindu culture, with the Bodo group of tribes becoming Aryan vassals during the Gupta period, except in certain pockets where they managed to continue to hold their own, with this region continuing to be known as the kingdom of Kamrupa and the most powerful kingdom of the east. The Bodos however managed to retain control over upper, central and south Assam, Manipur, Tripura and Garo Hills for quite sometime and called themselves Kamtapuris, Cacharis, Bodo – Cacharis, Dimasas, Meiteis, Tripuris and Garos in their respective areas, as did other hill tribes. During this period, the Aryans were consolidating their hold over areas they had moved into, there was a continued stream of further Tibeto-Burman migrations into upper Assam, Arunachal and Sikkim; this included Bodo sub-groups of Chutiyas, Lalungs, Misings, Lepchas and many other tribes.

## The Muslim Invasions

The kingdom of Kamrupa began disintegrating in the early 12$^{th}$ century after the fall of the Pala dynasty, with Kamtapur (Cooch Behar) separating from it, loss of control over a major part of upper Assam with the Mech and Chutiya Kingdoms coming into being. By this time Manipur and Tripura had also become independent kingdoms strongly influenced by Aryan culture.

After establishment of the Turk-Afghan rule at Delhi in the 12$^{th}$ century, the Sultanate turned their eyes eastwards for further conquests. Bihar and Bengal fell first. The Sultanate's Governor of Bihar and Bengal, Muhammad-Bin-Bakhtiyar Khilji, led the first expedition to conquer Kamrupa. They were, however, defeated on Kamtapur territory. The next expedition was launched in the early 13$^{th}$ century by the Sultanate's Governor of Bengal Ghiyasuddin Iwaz Khalji and was more successful as he managed to penetrate upto Nowgong in Assam – they were then, however, forced to retreat with heavy losses. The third expedition took place in the mid-13$^{th}$ century where they penetrated upto Guwahati but were again defeated and had to retreat – yet many of the invading Muslims settled in lower Assam and parts of Cooch Behar where their descendants can be found even today.

## Kuki – Chin Migrations

There were further mongoloid migrations through Myanmar into present day Mizoram, south Manipur and south Tripura by the Mizo and Kuki-Chin group of tribes. These were on account of nomadic movements resulting from famines in their original areas of habitation, in Chin Hills in Myanmar, consequent to flowering of bamboo and consequent ravages by rodents on all agricultural produce. They progressively took control over these new areas.

## The Ahoms and their Kingdom

In the 13$^{th}$ century, the Ahoms, reputedly a Shan tribe who were originally from Yunnan in China and who had migrated earlier to Myanmar, invaded upper Assam. As per the *Ahom Burunjis* (chronicles) they were initially led by a younger son of a Shan chieftain who had been banished by his tribe along with his followers – they progressively gained control and were perpetually in conflict with the Bodo groups. Due to a resurgence of the Bodos of lower Assam, the Aryan kings of Kamrupa were pushed out to Cooch Behar and later further west. The Bodos also gained control over south Bhutan and parts of Arunachal.

While the Ahoms were consolidating themselves, lower Assam was invaded by the Mughals (16th and 17th centuries) who had taken control of Bengal – they managed to gain control over parts of central and lower Assam for about 70 years, after which they were ultimately pushed back by the combined forces of the Ahoms and the other feudatory hill kingdoms and consequent to a great naval victory at Saraighat on the Brahmaputra near Guwhati. Groups of Mughal soldiers and their followers, however, settled in lower Assam building up on the existing Muslim pockets.

By the 17th century, the Ahoms had gained control over most of the plains of Assam with the exception of the Bodo pockets in lower, central (north of the Brahmaputra) and south Assam. They however failed to subjugate the hill tribes including those in Bhutan, who frequently raided Ahom and Bodo areas. They were kept under check through non-interference in the affairs of the hill tribes and punitive expeditions and raids launched by the border guarding forces of both the Ahom and Bodo kings whenever they carried out depredations against subjects of these kingdoms.

**Moamaria Insurgency**

By the 18th century consequent to the period of continuous war with the Mughals, Bodo kingdoms and local uprisings, there was very large-scale loss of life in the north-east resulting in its population getting denuded. Consequently the levies on manpower to fight these wars took its toll and agriculture, the basic mode of life of the common man, was adversely affected. Taxation became a very heavy burden resulting in a great deal of discontent. Further, the Ahom rulers who had started patronising the 'Shakti' cult of Hinduism persecuted the local population who had largely turned to Vaishnavism. When the persecution of the Vaishnavites became extreme, they revolted against the Ahom rulers and took up arms in the form of large-scale insurrection. This insurrection, known as the Moamariya revolt, spread across almost the entire Ahom kingdom but was most severe in the areas of the Marans and the Muttocks (Tinsukia, Dibrugarh and Sibsagar districts).

**Myanmar Intervention**

While dealt with very harshly by the Ahoms, quelling the insurrection took many decades with tremendous loss of life. As the Ahom troops were largely from the areas of the insurrection the Ahoms no longer trusted their own men – they therefore appealed to the Myanmar king at Ava for help. He responded promptly with an eye on colonising Assam and assisted the Ahoms in quelling the rebellion with extreme ruthlessness. The Myanmar troops ultimately left Assam with many thousand dead and took large numbers back with them into slavery.

The 18$^{th}$ and 19$^{th}$ centuries were the periods of misrule by the Ahoms. Thereafter, there was civil war amongst the Ahoms on matters of succession. Consequently this was a period of insurgency, strife and continuous conflict. The civil wars in the 19$^{th}$ century resulted in the Myanmarese being again invited to settle the disputes with consequent mass killing. Some chronicles indicate that during the period from the 17$^{th}$ to the early 19$^{th}$ century Assam was depopulated to the extent of about 70% due to strife and sickness.

The Myanmarese ultimately succeeded in occupying the Ahom dominions for two years before they were driven out. They were also at war with the Manipuris over matters of territory and payment of tribute around the same time.

## Relationship of Moamaria Insurgency to the ULFA Insurgency of Today

Interestingly the areas of insurgency and internal strife in Assam were the same as today – Tinsukia, Dibrugarh and Sibsagar were troubled areas during the period of the Moamaraih rebellions with support and sanctuary being offered by the Nagas of present-day Mon District and the Shan tribes in Myanmar Naga Hills. This remains the hotbed of ULFA activity in the region even now perhaps for the reason that the Marans and Muttocks who were the core of the Moamaria rebellions also form the core of the ULFA cadres.

## The Advent of the British

In the 19$^{th}$ century the British entered the scene on invitation of the Ahoms initially to help quell the civil war/insurgency in Assam and then again they were asked for help by the Ahoms and Manipuris in defeating the Myanmarese and pushing them out. After defeating the Myanmarese in 1824, the British progressively took control of the region. They then imposed an administration that supported imperial priorities and objectives of mercantile capitalism – to extract raw materials and wealth out of the colony. They developed rail, road and river infrastructure accordingly towards Chittagong and Calcutta. Tea plantations, coal, iron, other minerals and oil extraction were started.

**Instigated Migration and Subjugation of Hill Areas**
As Assam had been largely depopulated due to the strife and massacres, labour was imported from Bengal, Bihar and Uttar Pradesh, clerical/lower supervisory staff from Bengal and migration encouraged for cultivating land. By the end of the 19th century, the number of such migrants was over one hundred thousand. As the hill tribes were considered heathens, fierce warriors and potential threats and they frequently raided British facilities, the governing colonists attempted to subjugate them but found the process too costly, gave them partial autonomy and set about to civilise them through conversion to Christianity. To prevent depredations they inducted Kuki-Chin tribals from Chin Hills in Burma and settled them as a buffer between the Nagas and their colonies in Cachar and Manipur, thereby creating animosity between the tribes. To isolate the hill tribes from the politics of the plains, learnt bitterly from the experience of the 1857 uprising, they debarred migration of the plains' people into the hills and imposed what is today called the 'Inner Line', which ran along the base of the hills. Having brought in the Kuki-Chin tribes, they drew up administrative boundaries on the principle of 'divide and rule', resulting which communities were split by national and state boundaries. Present-day Arunachal was also segregated from the plains as part of their policy.

**Insertion of Nepalese**
By the 18th century, the Nepal's warring clans had come together under one rule. The Nepalese then attempted to expand their dominions through conquest and attempted to colonise Kumaon, Garhwal, Sikkim and part of Tibet which were then almost of British protectorate status. This led to conflict and subjugation of the Nepalese by the British. When the attempted colonisation by the Nepalese took place, a number of their soldiers and followers migrated and settled in these areas in large numbers. The British were so impressed by their bravery and valour that they started recruiting them into their Army in huge numbers and then used them as the primary force to bring the north-east under control. This automatically involved stationing Nepalese troops all over the north-east along with their followers and families

and their ultimately settling down in these areas and multiplying progressively.

## Bhutan's Tibetan Migrations and Regions adjoining the Brahmaputra valley

In the Middle Ages, Bhutan was invaded by the Tibetans in search of greener pastures. The Bodo-origin tribes who originally populated Bhutan were then driven out or assimilated by these invaders. This was followed by further Tibetan migrations. The invading tribes called themselves Drukpas. They then colonised the whole of Bhutan and attempted to expand southwards into Bengal and the Assam Duars where they came into conflict with the Ahoms, Bodos and Kamtapuris and subsequently the British. This led to conflict with the British who had by then colonised these areas. British subjugation of the Bhutanese in the 19$^{th}$ century using largely Nepalese troops, led to the Nepalese settling down in southern Bhutan in fairly large numbers and created today's Bhopali problem, i.e. the danger of demographic change with consequent clamping down on the migrant Nepalese (called Bhopalis). The British simultaneously colonised Myanmar. The Myanmar plains then were brought under direct administration and the hill areas given autonomy.

The British, due to a perceived Russian and Chinese threat, adopted a forward deployment policy in the 19$^{th}$ and 20$^{th}$ centuries and accordingly subjugated Tibet, Nepal, Bhutan, Sikkim and declared them protectorates to create a buffer zone. As Arunachal bordered Tibet they colonised Arunachal and subjugated of the tribes of Arunachal. As in the case of the other hill tribes of Naga and Mizo hills, they gave these tribes limited autonomy as well and an 'Inner Line' was imposed to try and prevent influence from the plains creeping in, following their experiences from the 1857 uprising.

## Effects of Migration

Migration of the current population thereby engineering serious demographic change is an issue of concern. In the early 20$^{th}$ century when Bengal was partitioned and Assam included in East Bengal, the majority of East Bengal migrants were Muslim. After the grant of provincial autonomy in 1935, the Muslim League was favoured by the British and with Saidullah as the Chief Minister of Assam, immigration of Muslims into Assam from East Bengal was encouraged. This was all the more so because the Muslim League prior to Partition had demanded that undivided Assam be included in East Pakistan. Even the Indian National Congress, much to Assam's chagrin, had accepted this. It was only due to rebellion by the Assam Congress that Assam was not included in erstwhile East Pakistan.

While figures quoted by various authorities are suspect, it is pertinent to note that in the 20$^{th}$ century under British rule, immigration and migration particularly into Assam, North Bengal and Tripura was probably to the extent of about 30% of their total census population, of which about two thirds were from East Bengal with the balance being from other areas. Unfortunately, after Independence this trend was allowed to continue, with the majority of migration being from the then East Pakistan. In 1971, again there was a major refugee exodus from East Pakistan into eastern India, the majority of whom never returned, due to the situation prevailing there, which ultimately led to the 1971 Indo-Pak war. Thereafter consequent to major agitations, particularly in Assam, immigration reduced but did not stop, primarily due to vote bank politics, wherein politicians for political gain encouraged this illegal migration. As people are now conscious of the consequent demographic changes, this illegal immigration/migration has now reduced to a comparative trickle.

The effects of this migration are – Tripura which had a tribal majority in the early 20$^{th}$ century is now a tribal minority state with a consequent long drawn insurgent movement by the tribals; Sikkim which earlier had a Lepcha and Bhutia majority now has a Nepalese majority; Assam today, has at least 30% of its population as Bangladeshi immigrants, with another 8–10% from Bengal, Bihar, UP and Rajasthan, which has changed its demographic profile and given birth to the Assam (ULFA), Bodo (NDFB and BLT), Karbi and Dimasa insurgencies; Assam now also has a minority Islamic fundamentalist movement, reduced per capita income and forest wealth; in North Bengal it gave rise to the Naxalite (Left extremist), Gurkha (GNLF) and Kamtapuri (KLO) movements, in Meghalaya it gave birth to the Khasi (HNLC) movement and the anti non Khasi agitations; and in other hill states harsh anti immigration policies. Whilst we may like to blame the British for these woes, the fact remains that maximum immigration has been post-Independence and that, in spite of knowing what was happening, both Delhi and the states failed to take suitable remedial action, which gave rise to widespread insurgency, strife, discontent, unnecessary commitment of security forces, with consequential excessive and wasteful expenditure to the state.

**Effects of Partition**
The partition of eastern India, with all created infrastructure passing through then East Pakistan totally disrupted both traditional and British rule trading patterns. East Pakistan being hostile, no routes were available except through the Siliguri corridor to the rest of India, with extremely indifferent communications – Chittagong was no longer available and Calcutta, the trade hub, was out on a limb – it became uneconomical to trade either with the rest of India or through Calcutta. Consequently both Calcutta's industry (which lost the East Bengal raw material and market) and Assam's (then comprising the entire North-East less Arunachal, Manipur, Tripura, Sikkim and North Bengal) fell into decay. Artificial boundaries created between India and Burma, split the Naga, Kuki-Chin-Mizo tribes and the Meities (Manipuris), coupled with pitting ethnic groups against each other and segregation of the hill people from the plainsmen, resulted in present-day problems of Naga, Mizo and Meitei demands for uniting their homelands and sowed the seeds of ethnic sub-nationalism and strife.

**Political Awakening**
The freedom struggle, partition movements, political changes in the world over, including the two World Wars and participation of people from the north-east in the same, the initial British defeat in World War II in South-East Asia and the north-east by the Japanese diluting the myth of British invincibility, and finally the promise of Indian independence – all played a significant role in shaping the political views of opinion-makers in India and the north-east region. The Partition policy-makers and the British having almost decided to give undivided Assam to East Pakistan is something that Assam and present-day Bangladesh have neither forgotten nor forgiven till date. Politically aware hill tribes were scared of assimilation into either the Hindu or Muslim homeland for fear of being totally overwhelmed, demanded freedom from the British and strengthened their determination to fight for it, if necessary.

Independence, with weak and inexperienced leadership and administration, coupled with communal violence and a bad economic situation in the north-east consequent to Partition, contributed along with the other factors to create a difficult environment. The British Forward Policy in trying to bring areas of Arunachal (NEFA) under direct control and independent India continuing with the same policy brought India into direct confrontation with the Chinese who also claimed these areas. The socialist movements and their success in Russia and China automatically enamoured and drew dissenters from the north-east into their fold. Chinese irritation with India over border disputes automatically resulted in their giving wholehearted support to such dissenting groups, which included insurgents from Naga and Mizo Hills and Manipur.

**Start of Insurgency in Nagaland, Manipur and Mizoram**
The late '50s saw the start of the Naga insurgency and commitment of security forces in the Naga Hills. The Meitei insurgency started at almost the same time, with the Lushai (Mizo) Hills insurgency starting a few years later. While each state's situation will be dealt with in subsequent chapters, it is important to note that the contributory factors were similar to those discussed above, coupled with acute mal-administration by an inexperienced Indian leadership. The insurgencies were sustained for long periods due to external support and power politics, public approbation, and the prevailing subversive environment all over South-East Asia. In this context, it is important to remember the particular ambience of the times – central and northern Burma was in flames, communist rebellions in Malaya, Vietnam, Cambodia and Laos were just starting, Chairman Mao's theories and socialism were the order of the day. India's quarrel with China led to the Indo-China war of '62 when US, through the CIA, was reportedly supporting the Tibetan insurgency against Chinese occupation of Tibet from Indian soil. Western support to India against China only strengthened China's determination to help the Indian insurgent groups. India's antagonism to Pakistan gave Pakistan the resolve to support these groups through East Pakistan joining hands with China.

India's subsequent alliance with Russia, who had fallen out with China during the Cold War, brought the West clandestinely into the fray against India. There was thus no dearth of external and environmental support (with neighbouring insurgent groups also providing sanctuary and aid) to the above insurgencies. Though after Mao's death, China has always claimed to have cut off this support; circumstances indicate that whenever we happen to have annoyed

China, there has been an upsurge of insurgency and whenever we have pleased them, insurgency has gone on a low key.

Pakistan and subsequently Bangladesh, after the death of Sheikh Mujibur-Rehman have always supported insurgencies in the north-east. After the Naga, Mizo and Meitei insurgencies, we have seen the birth of insurgency in Tripura, Assam, Arunachal and finally in North Bengal and Meghalaya.

This chapter has highlighted the effects of immigration, the British form of administration of the north-east, political awakening, partition of India, Independence, Indian administration, Chinese geo-political power politics and its contribution to the state of affairs in the north-east. In the next chapter, I will cover Assam and subsequently the other states.

# 2
# ASSAM

## General Overview

Undivided Assam, after British colonisation, was a huge state encompassing the entire north-east, excluding the erstwhile North-East Frontier tracts (present-day Arunachal and north-eastern Nagaland), Manipur, Tripura, Sikkim and North Bengal. Since Independence, it has been progressively split up into smaller states based broadly on ethnic grouping and now consists of:

- plains of the Brahmaputra valley,
- Karbi Anglong Plateau,
- plains of the Barak Valley,
- Cachar and North Cachar Hills,
- plains of Karimganj and Hailakundi districts bordering Bangladesh,
- It is enclosed on all sides by all the other north-eastern states with the exception of Sikkim and Bangladesh. Its unique geographic location – it sits astride the Brahmaputra and Barak river valley plains and has access to all north-eastern areas within it – makes it the hub and the core of the region.

## Population and Demography

Assam's population as per the 2001 census was 26,68,407. While details of the 2001 census are still not available, the 1991 census had:

- 67.13% Hindus,
- 28.48% Muslims,
- 2.4% Christians,
- 0.8% Budhists,
- 1.8% Sikhs,
- Balance undeclared

Assam's ethnic break-up is broadly:

- Assamese of Aryan origin 9%,
- Assamese of Ahom origin 10%,
- Assamese Muslims (pre-1901) 6%,
- Mongoloid tribals including Bodos 12%,
- Manipuris 2%,
- Nepalese 2%,
- Tea Tribes (*Adivasis*) 15%,
- Bangladeshi Muslims 22%,
- Bangladeshi Hindus 17%,
- Labour class from other parts of India 3%.

**Broad Religious Denominations**

The popular forms of Hinduism namely Saivism, Saktism and Vaishnavism are practised in the state. Neo-Vaishnavism gained momentum in the 16$^{th}$ century as a counter to Islam, under the leadership of Sankardeva and his disciple Madhavadeva. This cult drew its teachings from the Bhagwad Gita and is called *Mahapurushia Dharma*. *Satras* or Vaishnav monasteries were established bringing in a modified socio-cultural-intellectual lifestyle. More and more monasteries were progressively set up and this became the religion of the people with about 75% of the Hindus being part of this cult. Notwithstanding this, the Sakti movement had a strong following which included many Vaishnavites. Unlike many other parts of the country, Assamese are very liberal in their outlook towards religion.

The Muslims in Assam are generally called Gariyas (derived from Ghor – the original invaders). The descendants of Turbak's Army are called Mariyas. There are also many Syeds, Mughals, Khalifas and Pathans who are descendants of the Mughal army and their followers and religious teachers who came with them. Unlike the recent Bangladeshi Muslim migrants who still set themselves apart, these original Muslim settlers have been totally assimilated by the Assamese people – they have adopted the language, mode of living, social rites, superstitions and nationalistic views.

The Baptists are the most popular amongst the Christian denominations with the largest number of hill people following this faith, though some of them are still animists. Budhism also influenced in Assam in ancient times. The Khamtis, Phakials, Aitonias, Khamjangs, and Shyams still follow this religion. The Mughal armies brought a number of Sikhs with them who subsequently have been assimilated into the fabric of the state. In fact, it is recorded that both the Ahoms and Bodos recruited a large number of Sikhs into their armies. Jainism too has entered Assam in recent times primarily through Marwari traders.

## Language

The Assamese language is derived from the eastern version of Prakrit (Magadhi Apabhramsa) and has been enriched by Bengali, Austric, Kolerian, Malayan, Bodo and other languages and dialects. Bengali is also widely spoken in south Assam, while respective hill tribes use Bodo, Tai Ahom, Naga and their other own languages/dialects.

## General Problems of the State

Assam has a multitude of ethnic groups demanding autonomy due to socio-economic deprivation. Immigrants have swamped the state and migration, while reduced, continues – today its indigenous ethnic groups (400–500 years old or more) constitute only about 35 to 40% of its population. Whereas earlier Hindu predominant, it now has 28% Muslims. The state is also over-populated, as a large part of the area is flood plains with extensive floods every year, marshy, covered with tea gardens, oilfields, mines, and extensive reserved forests. Consequently there is a high population density in the available areas leading to food scarcity. The key reason for this could be an exploitative colonial-pattern economy – it continues to be mainly a primary-product-export region and a market for finished goods from other states. Assam has been repeatedly balkanised to create the neighbouring hill states, with each of whom it has problems – its people are not welcome in these states for fear of demographic change. While well-endowed with natural resources, the state lacks industry and markets and has tenuous lines of communication with the rest of India. In spite of being the hub of the region, it has got embroiled in insurgency and strife due to government neglect and mal-administration.

## Birth of the United Liberation Front of Assam (ULFA) and Insurgency in Assam

While there have been disturbances, agitation and riots by the people of Assam on the issues of immigration/migration, demographic change and language in the years 1951, 1960 and 1971, insurgency has its roots in the All Assam Students Union (AASU) movement of 1973. The

AASU felt that without agitation, the government would not listen to its demands. The movement started in Sibsagar (upper Assam) and spread like wildfire. In 1978, hardliners of the AASU created a military wing called United Liberation Front of Assam (ULFA) with the moderates forming a political party called All Assam Gana Sangram Parishad (AAGSP, now called AGP). The ULFA organised itself with the help of the Nationalist Socialist Council of Nagalim (NSCN), the ISI and Bangladeshi intelligence, creating a Robin Hood image by carrying out social work, and simultaneously organising itself into an insurgent group. Simultaneously, the AASU started agitations on immigration and connected issues. Attempts by the Election Commissioner and the Assam government to start identification of illegal immigrants and their deportation were opposed by those with vested interests – mainly political elements who were indulging in vote bank politics, in the form of encouraging migration with the aim of increasing their bank of votes. The Assam government resigned under public pressure over the issue, Presidents Rule was imposed and the Army called in.

In 1980 there were anti-Bengali and communal riots which had to be controlled by the Army. Talks were held between the AASU and the central government. The AASU's charter of demands included that illegal immigrants be identified on basis of the National Register of Citizens of 1951 and electoral rolls of 1952 (these are prepared by a body of the Census organization); all others be deported and further immigration be prevented. AASU efforts failed, as the central government would agree only to a post-1971 cut-off. The AASU started a blockade of the Siliguri Corridor, continuous agitation, coupled with ethnic and communal riots. The central government finally signed the Assam Accord in 1985, agreeing to a March 25, 1971 cut-off date coinciding with the birth of Bangladesh and agreed to issues of increasing investment and improvement in economic assistance to Assam. The Accord stipulated that all migrants who had settled in Assam on or before that date would be treated as Indian citizens and that all those who had entered the state after that date were to be detected and deported. Elections were then held and the AGP came into power. Since the Accord instructed the cut-off date as 1971, it did not meet aspirations of the hardliners – there was also no progress on implementation of the Accord or on identification or deportation of illegal migrants. From 1988 onwards, ULFA took control over Assam and launched a terror campaign with killings galore. In 1990, President's Rule was imposed again and the Army called in to control the situation. Within a short period, the situation was brought under partial control and a Congress government came into power. Again in a few months, the Army had to be called in to resume operations against the ULFA. This continued till 1995, when it was felt that the Army could be withdrawn. As the authorities had failed to address the basic issue of identification and deportation of illegal migrants or improvement of the economic situation, there was a revival of insurgency and the Army redeployed to execute counter-insurgency operations.

The ULFA initially headquartered itself in Assam, however as a result of continuous pressure from the Army and the police it shifted its headquarters to Bangladesh where it is located today. Media reports based on official releases by various agencies of the Indian government, my own experiences and reading on the issue indicate that the ULFA is funded through large-scale extortion carried out by its cadres in Assam from all and sundry and through large business enterprises that it has set up in Bangladesh with the help of the ISI and Bangladeshi intelligence. Its leadership leads a life of luxury in Bangladesh and is coerced by the ISI and Bangladeshi intelligence to do their bidding. ULFA had since inception been supported by Pakistan and Bangladesh and probably through them by China (based on circumstantial evidence covered in a subsequent chapter), who were prompting all insurgent groups of the north-east to demand secession.

**Bangladesh's Philosophy of Lebensraum**
It needs to be noted that it has always been East Pakistan's (and subsequently Bangladesh's) philosophy of 'Lebensraum', to encourage large-scale immigration that would result in a demographic change and engineer the entire north-east to secede to Bangladesh. To quote Bhutto in his book *Myth of Independence*, 'It would be wrong to assume that Kashmir is the only dispute between India and Pakistan.... One is nearly as important as the Kashmir dispute, that of Assam and some districts in India adjacent to East Pakistan. To these Pakistan has very good claims.' The philosophy of 'Lebensraum' has been enunciated openly by a large number of Bangladeshi authorities including Sheik Mujibur Rehman who wrote in *East Pakistan – its Population and Economics*', 'because East Pakistan must have sufficient land for its expansion and because Assam has abundant natural resources etc, East Pakistan must include Assam'. Sadeek Khan, a former diplomat

stated in his article in *Holiday*, (Dhaka, 18 Oct 1991) 'All projections indicate that by the next decade Bangladesh would face a serious crisis of Lebensraum…a natural overflow of population pressure is very much on the cards and will not be restrained by barbed wire or border patrols. A natural trend of population overflow from Bangladesh is towards the sparsely populated lands in the south-east, in the Arakan side and in the North East of the Seven Sisters of the Indian sub-continent'.

## *Effects of Bangladesh's Philosophy on ULFA*

With Bangladesh supporting the ULFA, it would therefore be apparent that the ULFA has totally lost sight of its original anti-immigration philosophy and the 'protector of the people image' and is now merely a tool in the hand of foreign powers to wage proxy war against India in Assam.

## **Bhutan Operations**

While insurgency was kept under control by the Army, the ULFA, whose bases were in Bangladesh, Myanmar and Bhutan, was under pressure from Bangladesh and Pakistan to step up their operations particularly during the Kargil war and thereafter. Diplomatic parleys were therefore held with the Royal Bhutan Government, who agreed to throw the ULFA out of Bhutan. These operations were launched in 2004 by the Royal Bhutan Army and led by the King of Bhutan personally; Indian Army's role was to execute border-sealing operations on their side of the border. The operation was a resounding success with ULFA and all other insurgent groups in Bhutan being thrown out. Efforts are now on by the central government to try and get Myanmar and Bangladesh to follow suit – though so far there has been little success. Over the last one year the ULFA has tried its best to recuperate from the loss of the large part of its men and material in Bhutan sanctuary and has been trying to make its presence felt again through a series of bomb blasts all over Assam. The situation is however under control. As a result of these operations and public pressure on ULFA for peace, they have now started parleys for talks with the Government of India. One can only hope that good sense prevails and that peace would return to Assam after such a long period of violence and strife.

### Effects of the ULFA Insurgency on other Ethnic Groups

The ULFA and ASSU movements encouraged other minority groups to agitate for socio-economic improvements, autonomy and removal of illegal immigrants. Assam has now witnessed long drawn rebellions by almost all tribes of Bodo origin, the Karbis, and Kukis (Kuki National Army – KNA). As a result of these movements, the Dimasas and Karbis have been given limited autonomy and talks with the governments of Assam and the centre are in progress to try and resolve their grievances. Ceasefire agreements have also been arrived at and have been implemented between the Government of India and a faction of the insurgents of each of these two ethnic groups (Dima Halim Dauga – DHD and United Peoples Democracy Solidarity – UPDS). The problems in general however persist, as the causes have not been addressed. Let us now take an overview of the Bodo insurgency, reasons for which are quite different from that of the ULFA.

### The Bodo Movement

The Bodos had started an autonomy movement prior to Independence on account of their perception that the Assamese were exploiting them. They had periodically agitated for the same through the All Bodo Students Union (ABSU) and demanded a separate state called Udayachal. In 1980, they restated this demand. The hardliners amongst the Bodos then formed Bodo SF as an insurgent group in 1986 that started insurgency in 1990. Initial aims were for separate statehood. The Army was deployed to deal with the Bodo SF. In 1993 it was agreed that a Bodo Autonomous Council (BAC) would be formed on the north bank of the Brahmaputra for the Bodos. This decision resulted in a split amongst the Bodos with formation of the Bodo Liberation Tigers (BLT), who favoured peaceful resolution; and the National Democratic Front of Bodoland (NDFB) (old Bodo SF) who were hardliners – the NDFB then joined hands with ULFA, took sanctuary in Bhutan and Bangladesh, and demanded secession. The BAC proposals fell through. The NDFB is also headquartered in Bangladesh and its source of funding is through extortion. After a fairly long period of insurgency it was the Bhutan operations, wherein the NDFB was severely mauled, that have largely contributed towards nudging the hardliners towards talks. The All Bodo Students Union (ABSU) and BLT with the present government have now negotiated a

Bodo Autonomous Region and it is hoped that it would come through shortly. Should this not for any reason happen, insurgency would possibly resume.

### *Likely Effects of the Bodo Accord*
It must be noted that this approach by the authorities is fraught with dangers, as the Bodos form only about 30–40% of the population of the proposed 'Bodo Autonomous Region'. The other ethnic groups, which include the Rajbangshis, Rabhas and Koches, the Tea Tribes, Assamese, Bangladeshi migrants amongst others, form the balance 60–70% of the population and are already agitating against this. This is coupled with the fact that some of these ethnic groups are now joining hands with people of the same ethnic origin in West Bengal to demand similar concessions from the government and to stall the Bodo Accord. There is therefore every likelihood of strife in the future.

### *Ceasefire with NDFB*
The recent ceasefire agreement arrived at between the Government of India and the NDFB, is also a welcome development – the situation however needs to be watched closely particularly as the leadership of the NDFB is controlled by the ISI and DGFI.

### **The Illegal Migrants Determination Tribunals Act**
The recent striking down of the Illegal Migrants Determination Tribunals Act (IMDT) (which was instituted by the government after the Assam Accord), by the Supreme Court of India has vindicated Assamese views on the issue of migration. The IMDT Act placed the onus of proof of citizenship on the authorities which made it difficult to prove that the individual was an illegal migrant. As the Act has now been set aside, the Foreigners' Act would now apply all over the country. This places the responsibility of proof of citizenship on the individual which would make identification simpler. While this is indeed heartening, it would be now definitely easier to identify and deport foreigners, there still has to be political will to do so – whether this will really improve the situation is yet to be seen.

### **Ethnic Strife in South Assam**
A clear policy also needs to be formulated by the authorities for handling the affairs of south Assam, which has large tracts claimed by the National

Socialist Council of Nagalim (NSCN) as part of 'Greater Nagaland'. Many of these areas are currently inhabited by Nagas, Kukis, Manipuris, Hmars, Karbis, Dimasas and Bodos. These claims and the attempts by the NSCN to enforce them by forcible occupation have led to strife between these ethnic groups that threaten to escalate out of hand. The government also has to decide on how to deal with the predominantly Bengali-speaking belt of Cachar, Hailakundi and Karimganj, which continue to indicate high Bangladeshi immigration patterns.

**Action Required by the Authorities**
While the aspects of what needs to be done towards the problem resolution in Assam will be covered in detail holistically in subsequent chapters, in a nutshell, it needs to be noted that with good governance, concentration on all-round economic development, grass-root autonomy catering to the needs of all ethnic groups, Assam's problems are not insurmountable. This is particularly as the people are tired of violence and desperately want peace. Notwithstanding this, ULFA hardliners continue to extort funds from the state and try to impose their dictates from the sanctuaries in Bangladesh, with support from Bangladesh and Pakistani intelligence agencies. Denial of this external support and the issue of opening up trade routes through Bangladesh to assist in resolution of Assam's economic woes, need to be dealt with urgently by the central government.

# 3
# NAGALAND

**Location, Demography and History**

Nagaland astrides the Patkai and Naga hill ranges of the eastern hills. It has Arunachal and Assam to its north, Myanmar to its east, Manipur to its south and Assam to its west. It has about 20 resident tribes (14 major), conjointly called Nagas.

As per the 2001 census, the population is 1,988,636.

The approximate but pertinent tribal break-up is:

- Angami 9%,
- Ao 15%,
- Chakesang 8%,
- Chang 2%,
- Khiamniungan 2%,
- Konyak 15%,
- Lotha 7%,
- Phom 3%,
- Rengma 1.5%,
- Makware 0.5%,
- Sangtam 4%,
- Sema 13%,
- Tikhir 0.5%,
- Yimchunger 2%,
- Zeliang 2%,
- Garos 1%,
- Chir/BodoKachari/Kuki/Mikir/others 16%.

The origin of the term 'Naga' is obscure – it is used to identify tribes living in the Naga Hills. Nagaland has no recorded history other than some folklore documented by the British and Indian authorities who served or travelled in Nagaland such as Verrier Elwin, Lt Gen S K Pillai, PVSM (Retired), Bob Kathing, N F Suntook, a few references to them in the Ahom Chronicles, passing references in Hindu epics, and aspects of folklore related by people in Nagaland. Folklore and anthropological studies indicate the tribes migrated from the general area of Yunnan, before the birth of Christ. Each of these tribes settled into separate areas in the Naga Hills and has throughout been antagonistic to each other.

## Their Characteristics and Values

These tribes are ethnically, culturally and ideologically distinct from valley people and in most cases from each other. They have enjoyed tribal autonomy and any threat to their fierce individuality invites violent reaction. The Bodos, Ahoms, Mughals, Manipuris, Myanmarese and the British found it expensive to subjugate them. They therefore followed the core-fringe philosophy of administration – entering into agreements with various tribes to maintain peace by allowing them autonomy; and whenever they did not do so, to conduct punitive operations against them.

Till the 19th century, Naga beliefs were primordial and animistic as they were relatively untouched and isolated from civilization. Their entire system was based on superstitious beliefs in animistic worship and rites. Their world was built around their family, their clan, their village and their traditional rights to the land they lived on, cultivated and hunted in (may be about 30 to 40 sq km). The women attended to household chores and the duty of the men was to provide for the family through hunting and protecting the traditions and rights of the clan. Decisions were made mainly through councils of elders nominated by the clan, except in a few tribes, where the concept of chieftains prevailed.

The family and clan came first and foremost and they would war with neighbouring clans' villages when they felt that another clan had infringed on their rights. On major issues the clans banded together as a tribe to enforce and protect their values. Headhunting was the order of the day till as late as the mid 20th century. Being a good warrior was what all young men aspired for. The village and clan therefore had total autonomy in their affairs. Visits to areas outside their tribal boundaries except for limited barter trade or for raiding expeditions were very limited. It is due to this that their values subsisted in the simple philosophy of 'tribe – land – village – autonomy'.

The sudden transition from 'tradition to modernity', that came with rapid conversion to Christianity, in these parts, along with concepts of westernisation and interaction with other communities, have not yet been adapted to very well. Even today, a Naga who wears a suit, can read the Bible and speak English, his clan and his tribe are still first and foremost priority and any slight to them demands retribution. How can he forget that another tribe had killed his clansmen or taken away his people as slaves barely fifty to a hundred years ago? It is due to this that there is still a great deal of animosity among the tribes and sub-tribes and even more so against the people of the plains who they perceive as threats to their value system. There is also the issue of looking different from the plains' people. To my mind, modernity can only be achieved through education and motivation spread over a long period of time.

## The British Policy

Under British rule the Nagas were allowed local autonomy as subjugation was found to be too expensive and the 'Inner Line policy' enunciated to keep them aloof from political awakening. The 'Inner Line Regulation' was promulgated in 1873 – this restricted contact of outsiders with the Naga tribes. The world was told that this was to protect the local from exploitation, mainly from traders. In reality, it was a step taken to prevent the politics of the plains that the British had experienced from the 1857 uprising affecting the Naga tribes. This system was reiterated in the 'Home Rule Regime' promulgated vide the Government of India Act 1935 in which Naga Hills District was declared an 'Excluded Area'. The British tried to civilise them through conversion to Christianity and western values and culture. The effect was to partially weld them together in a fashion that no administration could ever achieve. Christianity meant literacy – to be able to read scriptures and adopt western dress and lifestyles, but it did not change their basic value system.

## The Issue of Identity and Ethnicity

Broadly speaking, identity is defined by sociologists as the collective sum of the unique qualities and beliefs of people, whereas ethnicity is considered to be the sense of belonging to a definable group of people with a common origin and ancestry. This concept was used by A.Z. Phizo, the legendary Angami Naga insurgent leader to try and get the Naga tribes to band together to meet the threat of being swamped by plainsmen, culturally and economically, if they were to remain with India. In reality this is not a truism. The Kukis were also once considered to be Nagas and a Kuki was a signatory to the Memorandum submitted by the Naga Club in 1929 to the Simon Commission. The Naga Club was a group of 20 Nagas (composed primarily of Phizo's Angami friends with representation from only six of the Naga tribes and one Kuki) who made a representation against being bracketed with India. Today the Kukis are vehemently considered by the Naga tribes to be non-Nagas and an ethnic group to be put down by force of arms. Similarly, many of the Nagas of Nagaland do not consider the present-day Manipuri Nagas to be true Nagas, despite the fact it is the Manipuri Nagas who form the preponderance of the National Socialist Council of Nagalim – Muivah (NSCN (I&M)), which in turn controls most of Nagaland. The Manipuri Nagas too do not consider many of the Myanmar Nagas to be true Nagas.

In the 19th and early 20th centuries, there was no generic consciousness amongst the proclaimed Naga tribes. It is also mentioned in the memorandum submitted to the Simon Commission – 'We have different languages which cannot be spoken by each other…. We have no unity amongst us and it is only the British Government that is keeping us together.' While there was a partly common bond, tribes and villages traditionally fought each other in the way that the Indian princely states fought each other though tied together by a common culture. This remains so even today with tribal loyalties always coming first.

There is a considerable debate about the number of Naga tribes. Though originally an anthropological issue, today it is political. Generally the working figure is 35 Naga tribes of which 20 are in Nagaland (the 1991 census indicated 17 and earlier to that it was 14 – the numbers have increased due to ethnic politics). The remainder lives in Manipur, Arunachal Pradesh, Assam and Myanmar. According to the NSCN (I&M), Nagaland extends to the River Chindwin in Myanmar; covers almost the entire Manipur; Cachar and North Cachar Hills and the Disturbed Area belt in Assam; Tirap, Changlang and Lohit districts in Arunachal Pradesh – but excluding the Kuki-Chin-Mizo belt in south Manipur – a huge area with a population of near 3 million. This is indeed a very difficult demand which cannot be met as giving in would amount to separating a large number of other ethnic groups from their primary treasure —'land'.

Two surprising aspects of claimed Naga ethnicity stand out – first is the total lack of a common language. Even today people of different Naga tribes and even clans can speak to each other only through

Nagamese (Assamese tinged by a smattering of words of different dialects) or English. The second issue is one of origin – despite claims of migration from South-East Asia/China which are broadly accepted, none of the tribal myths indicate migration from distant regions or from a common motherland. Anthropological evidence indicates ethnic differences between tribes and indeed some Negrito blood in a few of them. Notwithstanding these facts, Naga ethnicity has been progressively built up through a series of developments in recent times, most important of which was the policy of "Inner Line" politics which the British had adopted. Ethnicity was also built up by setting up of the Naga Club in 1918 and the Ao and Lotha Tribal Councils in 1928. In 1929, the Naga Club had presented their memorandum to the Simon Commission. Thereafter a Naga Hills District Tribal Council was formed. This became a semi-political organisation as awareness of the Indian and Myanmar independence movement grew.

## Political Awakening and Demands for Independence

These events led to political awakening, which coupled with exposure to the World Wars, collapse of the British Empire, partition of the sub-continent; British proposals to reconstitute the hill districts as a 'Crown Colony'; successful prosecution of guerrilla war against the Japanese further politicised them and reinforced demands for independence. Indian independence threatened loss of their culture, values and traditional administrative institutions. The new Indian leadership decided to continue with the British policy of administration – autonomy and segregation. This only alienated them, prevented their assimilation into the mainstream; reinforced their feeling of being different and superior to the plains' people and facilitated interaction with their brethren in Myanmar, who had taken up arms against their government with similar demands. Mal-administration and lack of development; attempt by the Assam government to enforce Assamese as the state language, witnessing the flood of Bangladeshi migration only added to their fears.

In 1946 the Naga Hills Tribal Council was converted into the Naga National Council (NNC) – it had 29 members but was not representative of the majority of the Naga tribes – it became a dominant minority, which from then onwards profoundly influenced Naga aspirations. Even within the NNC, there were differing views – some favoured independence, some autonomy within India, and others a protectorate status. All Naga government servants who in actual fact formed the majority of the Naga intelligentsia were banned by the government from participation in the NNC, consequently Phizo's views prevailed. No attempts were made to allay the Naga fears or crucial issues raised by them.

In 1947 immediately after the Independence, a Nine-Point Agreement was signed between the Government of Assam and the NNC, wherein considerable autonomy was granted to the Nagas but this did not meet their satisfaction. There were also ambiguous clauses in the Agreement to the effect that the arrangement would be reviewed after 10 years. The Agreement had not been cleared by the Assembly, which made the Nagas distrustful of the government's motives. Phizo unilaterally declared Naga independence from India in August 1947 as the self-proclaimed representative of the Nagas. There was then a power struggle in the NNC ranks between the moderates led by Aliba Imti and Phizo and their followers. Ultimately Phizo won the battle in 1950 and was proclaimed the President of the NNC. In 1951 Phizo organised a controversial plebiscite in Naga Hills District to determine whether the Nagas wanted independence or a merger with India. He then claimed that 99% were in favour of independence. In fact, the so-called plebiscite was held only in Kohima and Mokokchung with limited attendance, and women and other areas of Nagaland had been excluded. These realities are little known to all including the Naga public at large. Notwithstanding these facts, it is unfortunate that the authorities ignored this plebiscite, consequently total alienation progressively set in.

**Start of Insurgency**
Hostilities started between the insurgents and the government forces from 1953 with the belligerents declaring themselves the 'Peoples Sovereign Republic of Free Nagaland'. This led to insurgency and deployment of Security Forces (SF) in the State. Violence then increased. In 1955 the Naga Federal Government replaced this. By 1955 there was a rift between Phizo's extremists and the moderates and inter-factional assassinations commenced with all those opposed to Phizo being targeted. Successful counter insurgency operations forced Phizo to flee to Dacca with Reverend Michael Scott's help, where they received Pakistani assistance and thereafter to London. Between 1957

and 1960, there were three Naga People's Conventions held in Nagaland, which were very well-attended and sought peaceful resolution of the problem. These progressively contributed to the Government of India agreeing to a 16-Point Proposal by them and the state of Nagaland coming into being and Tuensang district of NEFA was merged with it. Notwithstanding these events, insurgency continued. The problem was aggravated by Chinese and Pakistani support to the movement.

Unfortunately both the Governments of India and Nagaland disregarded advice that the political structure should be derived from the existing traditional Naga system of governance and internal polity. Instead the structure existing in the other states was imposed with a top-heavy structure and a totally bloated bureaucracy, which has contributed to loss of Naga identity, lack of adequate representation of all the ethnic groups, corruption and poor governance.

**The Shillong Accord**
The administration gained respite in the post-1971 period, due to successful prosecution of counter insurgency operations which forced the hostile bands to flee to Myanmar; and reduced Chinese support to the insurgents. The creation of Bangladesh and therefore non-availability of Pakistani bases and support in that country helped as did the Shillong Accord of 1975, wherein the NFG and NNC accepted the Indian Constitution and agreed to lay down their arms.

**Birth of the NSCN**
The respite was however short-lived due to the coup and military rule in Bangladesh, with consequent renewed support from Pakistan, China and Bangladesh and sanctuary in Myanmar; the birth of the National Socialist Council of Nagalim (NSCN) out of the anti-Shillong Accord factions, and adoption of a common cause with Myanmar insurgents. The 80s witnessed a split in the NSCN, partially on ethnic lines and a blood feud leading to a power struggle between the two factions of the NSCN – the Issac & Muivah (I&M) and Khaplang (K) groups (named after the leaders) to gain control over Nagaland and Naga-inhabited areas in Manipur, Assam and Arunachal (then known as NEFA). There were also changes in the pattern of insurgency. NSCN (I&M)'s Pakistani mentors managed to convince its members that success was feasible only if they operated conjointly with other insurgent groups and that

their philosophy needed to change to secession of the entire north-east! This led to NSCN (I&M) becoming the mother organisation of most of the insurgent groups in the region.

## The Ceasefire

Due to successful SF operations, NSCN (I&M) was forced out of Nagaland by the late '90s to bases in adjoining states and countries where they received sanctuary, which included Bangladesh, Myanmar and Thailand. It was due to these operations and public pressure that they were forced to ask for a ceasefire which has been in place since 1997. At that stage NSCN (K) controlled most of Nagaland and parts of the Naga inhabited areas in the adjoining states as well. A ceasefire was similarly brokered with the NSCN (K). The NSCN (K) was headquartered in Myanmar adjacent to Tirap and Changlang Districts of Arunachal. The ceasefire applied to both the NSCN groups but is officially applicable only to Nagaland, as other state governments refused to agree to demands for 'Greater Nagaland', wherein large chunks of Manipur, Assam and Arunachal were claimed. In reality, the SF rarely operate against the NSCN (I&M) outside Nagaland, to obviate talks breaking down, which had been initiated by Government of India with NSCN (I&M) only.

## Talks between Government of India and NSCN (I&M)

With the ceasefire in place in Nagaland, talks have been in progress for sometime between the Government of India and the NSCN (I&M). This is apparently on account of the fact that NSCN (I&M) cadres are primarily Indian Nagas, and are considered to be the mother insurgent group of the north-east. It however needs to be noted that almost all the NSCN (I&M) leadership and at least 40% of their cadres are from the Tangkhul Tribe of the Nagas in Manipur and not Nagaland, with another 40% being from other Manipuri, Assamese and Arunachali Naga tribes – not more than 10–15% or less of the cadres are from the Nagaland tribes. This is because the Naga tribes living outside Nagaland feel the majority communities in their home states are exploiting them and that they have been socially, economically and politically deprived. As against this, the NSCN (K) has its cadres mainly from the Myanmar Naga tribes and the tribes located in areas that they control. It is because the leadership of the NSCN (K) and some of its cadres are not Indian Nagas and its power is on the wane, that the Government of India have not initiated talks with NSCN (K). It is for this reason that many of the Nagaland Naga tribes, NSCN (K) and other groups, view these talks with suspicion, distrust and scepticism, as they consider the Government of India negotiations with the I&M to be talks with the Tangkhuls of Manipur, who are not considered to be Nagas by many of the Nagas of Nagaland and are trying to lord over them by force of arms.

## Activity during Ceasefire

The people, who are tired of violence, have used the period of the ceasefire, to propagate peace. The NSCN groups have used the ceasefire to consolidate their hold over areas, strengthen themselves and eliminate their rivals. Elections have also been held and a new government has come into place, which are keen to make the cease-fire and the talks succeed. Due to the importance given to them, the NSCN (I&M) has more or less gained control over the entire state by force, with exception of the north-east which remains under NSCN (K) control. While there are popular pressures for rapprochement of both groups, this is currently unlikely due to ethnic rivalry and blood feuds.

The NSCN (I&M) is the strongest insurgent group today, which has expanded to over 5000 cadres and is well-equipped and armed with the latest modern weapons. It calls the shots in the region, dictates terms to most other insurgent groups, runs a parallel government and administration, collects taxes from all in both Nagaland and its claimed areas of Greater Nagaland (including from government servants). The NSCN (I&M) has quite obviously prepared itself for an eventuality of the ceasefire breaking down.

## Summation of Causes of Naga Discontent

Let us now take a look at the causes of alienation of the Nagas and relate these to current Naga demands:
- Traditional tribal society of the many Naga ethnic groups feel culturally, socially and religiously overwhelmed and economically exploited by the people of Hindu India. In spite of the Sixth Schedule of the Indian Constitution, having been so well-framed to cater towards protection of the culture, values and traditions of the minorities, the foisting of the Indian political structure, with its inherent inadequacies on the Nagas, was seen as an imposition and served as a cause for alienation.

- Creation of political boundaries including that of Nagaland, split traditional territorial areas of the tribes disrupted social interaction and traditional forms of economic activity and trade.
- With passage of time, the political structure (majority rule) and boundaries resulted in denial of development and employment prospects for the minority hill tribes in Manipur, Arunachal and Assam.
- The Accord of 1974 satisfied only those ethnic elements which benefited by the majority rule. The Naga tribes which were left out, such as those in Myanmar, Arunachal, Assam, Manipur and those in minority, were aggrieved by the Accord and formed the NSCN. Ethnic distrust and blood feuds led to a further split in the form of the 'K' and 'I&M' groups of the NSCN.

## Demands of NSCN (I&M)

It is this background that has led to the current charter of demands {primarily from NSCN (I&M)}, the more important being of sovereignty (implying a very high degree of autonomy to run their society as they choose), and for creation of 'Nagalim' or Greater Nagaland for the Nagas residing outside Nagaland, including the areas in Manipur, Assam and Arunachal. There are however indications that the NSCN (I&M) may agree to compromise on the issue of sovereignty if given a high degree of autonomy. Their demands also include a separate flag, a role in foreign policy, economic aspects and defence besides other less important issues. Naturally, all the adjoining states vehemently oppose this.

## Demands of the People of Nagaland

As opposed to the above, the people of Nagaland are simply asking for peace with honour —this implies autonomy and freedom to lead their own lives in accordance with the values of their particular ethnic groups – these are clearly different to NSCN (I&M) demands.

## Likely Effects in case the Government Agrees with NSCN (I&M)

It should be noted that much of the ailment in Manipur, Assam and Arunachal stems from the demands of NSCN (I&M). While over a period of time there has been some rapprochement between the Naga ethnic groups, strong inter-ethnic group rivalry and clashes are likely in the foreseeable future. Those involved in policy formulation and talks with the Government of India, need to comprehend that coming to an agreement with only NSCN (I&M) will be seen as having done a deal with the Tangkhuls, which may be unacceptable to the vast majority of tribes, people and the states. Such an agreement is therefore unlikely to succeed. Further, acceptance of some of the demands would amount to acceptance of balkanisation of the Indian Union. Notwithstanding the above, due to public pressure there has been relative peace in Nagaland for the last seven years. One can only hope and pray that a lasting and acceptable solution be found to the problem.

In this chapter we have attempted to familiarise readers with a background of the Naga problem, the situation as it stands today and a frank assessment of the peace process including the issues involved and its future prospects. One cannot and must not delve into the aspect of problem resolution for Nagaland alone – this unfortunately is the error that is repeatedly being made by those in authority. Any attempt to do so would be disastrous as it involves compromising on core issues of the neighbouring states and countries. The aspect of problem resolution is therefore covered in the subsequent chapters after considering all possible issues encompassing the region as a complete entity. Resolution essentially lies in the field of socio-politics as explained later. In the next chapter, we will see how the prevalent problems of Manipur are closely linked to Naga and Mizo issues.

# 4
# MANIPUR

**Location, Demography and Situation**
Manipur is a beautiful valley and in many ways similar to Kashmir. It sits astride the Patkai, Naga and Manipur hill ranges – it has Nagaland to the north, Myanmar to the east, Mizoram to the south and Assam to the west. About 75 % of the state is hilly with the hills surrounding the valley on all sides. The valley is about 70 km long and 35 km wide. The hill tribes inhabit the hills and the Meiteis the plains. The 2001 census declared its population to be 23,88,634.

## *Demographic profile*

- Naga Tribes – Ao, Kabui, Angami, Zeliang, Khongazai, Mao, Tangkhul – 13%
- Kuki-Chin-Anal, Chiru, Chothe, Gangte, Koira, Kom, Lamgang, Mizo, Mansang, Paite, Ralte, Sahte, Simte, Thadou, Vaiphei, Zou – 14%
- Meitei – 58%
- Others – 15% (including Muslims)

The seven main Naga tribes of Manipur have a number of sub-tribes and clans. The main tribes however are dissimilar to each other in many respects including aspects of language and dialect and have throughout history been hostile to each other. Out of the Naga tribes listed above it are only the Aos, Zeliangs and the Angamis that spill across the boundary into Nagaland. Though considered part of the Naga tribes by the authorities, many of the Nagaland Naga tribes do not accept the Manipuri Nagas as being part of them. The Nagas resident in Manipur however universally feel neglected by the Meiteis on issues of economy, jobs, development, culture and governance and strongly feel that the Meiteis have wrongfully seized their lands and sources of livelihood. They similarly feel that the forcible settlement of the Kuki-Chin tribals on their lands by the British was wrong. They further believe that the Government of India has supported the other ethnic groups against their interests, which have further alienated them. The issues of both identity and ethnicity are therefore even more pronounced than Nagaland. They have joined together in an alliance in the form of the NFG, NSCN (K) or the NSCN (I&M) (opposed to each other in ideology and ethnic grouping) to forcibly try and resolve their problems.

The Kuki-Chin-Mizo tribes reside in a number of different pockets in Manipur. The majority is located in south Manipur in the districts of Chandel and Churachandpur adjacent to Mizoram. There are however two pockets in district Senapati sandwiched between the Maos, Zeliangs, Tangkhuls and the Meiteis and some in Imphal. While broadly of the same ethnic group, there is a great deal of sub-tribe rivalry primarily between the Kukis, Hmars, Paites, Zous, Zomis, Mizos, derived from the fact that Mizos get preferential treatment in Mizoram and that the demand of the non-Mizo, Kuki-Chin tribal group for inclusion in Mizoram and demands for Greater Mizoram are perceived not to have been pressed adequately. There is also the perception that the Mizos have not aided the Kuki-Chin minorities in Manipur adequately as a result of which they have suffered tremendously at the hands of both the Nagas and the Meiteis. Consequently we have a nascent insurgent movement by the non-Mizo, Kuki-Chin groups which are antagonistic to all other ethnic groups including the Mizos.

The Meiteis reside primarily in the valley floor of Manipur extending up to Moreh and along the Bishenpur axis into Cachar district of Assam. They consider themselves superior to all the other ethnic groups in Manipur intellectually, culturally and in all other related aspects. They feel they are being oppressed to meet the demands of the tribes inhabiting in the hills and are antagonistic towards them.

**Inter-Ethnic Conflict**

Manipur therefore has inter-ethnic conflict among the Naga tribes; Meitei (Manipuri) and Naga tribes (residing in the north, west and eastern hills of Manipur valley), Kuki-Chin tribals versus both the Nagas and the Meiteis, between the ethnic sub-groups of the Kuki-Chin-Mizo tribals, demands for Greater Nagaland and Mizoram or 'valley' (Meitei) versus 'hill' inhabitants. This is consequent to political, social, geographic, historical and economic instability, emanating from fragmentation and fractionalisation of polity and society, due to acute mal-administration and neglect. Today, Manipur is in a state of total anarchy where the writ of the Indian government simply does not run – the situation in the state is much worse than in any other part of the country. It remains out of the media headlines only on account of the fact it is so far away from Delhi and mainstream Indian politics and that no one including the media is bothered about the state.

**History**

Historically the Meiteis (anthropologically their origin is from the Bodo group of tribes), who occupy the valley floor are the most populous ethnic group in the state, and have ruled the state for a long period – their kingdom reportedly stretched from river Brahmaputra in the north, to river Chindwin (now in Myanmar) in the south around the period of the birth of Christ. Manipur plains are the core and the surrounding hills are the fringe regions. Hill tribes were permitted local autonomy, subject to their maintaining peace and giving tribute to kings of Manipur. After Aryan migrations into Bengal, the Meiteis became strongly influenced by Hinduism and Vedic culture. In the 16$^{th}$ century, they adopted Vaishnavism and became powerful in the region, along with the Bodo Cacharis who ruled from Dimapur, Mughals who ruled Bengal, Tripuris and Ahoms. From then onwards, the kings of Myanmar who wished to expand their territory subjected them to repeated invasions. The power struggle with the Bodo, Cacharis and other powers of the region also took its toll. The Manipuri population was decimated and economy disrupted. Consequently, they were neither able to keep the hill tribes under control, nor the invading Myanmar hordes at bay. In 1824, they appealed to the British for help. The British defeated the Myanmarese, but forced Manipur to cede to Myanmar the rich Kabaw Valley. They also instigated massive migrations of Kuki-Chin-Mizo tribes, to act as a buffer between the Nagas and their plantations in the Cachar, into south Manipur (Churachandpur and Chandel districts) and parts of central Manipur with a view to stop the Naga tribes from raiding their newly set up colonies and plantations.

Thus relations between the British and Manipuris deteriorated, leading to the 1891 Anglo-Manipur war and British annexation of the state. There was political awakening and participation in India's freedom struggle, with many Meiteis supporting the Japanese and joining the Indian National Army against the British. After Partition, the Maharaja of Manipur acceded to the Indian union, which evoked insurgency amongst Naga and Meitei groups who wanted independence. It needs to be recollected at this stage that the wave of Mao's socialist philosophy was sweeping across the whole of East and South-East Asia. The newly created Manipur Communist party then reached an understanding with Myanmar communists, who with Chinese backing had control over the adjoining areas in Myanmar, to cede the Kabaw Valley back to Manipur, in return for creation of an independent socialist state of Manipur that would ally it to the Chinese communists. In the '50s-'60s, due to perceived Meitei exploitation a number of Manipur Naga tribals joined the Naga movement. Shortly thereafter, as the Mizo insurgency in Mizoram had just started, many Kuki-Chin-Mizo tribals joined their counterparts in Chin and Mizo Hills and started agitating that the Kuki-Chin-Mizo belts in Manipur be merged with Mizo Hills. They also engaged in inter-ethnic depredations for control of south Manipur around Moreh bordering Myanmar and the lucrative trans-border drug and other smuggled goods' trade to fund their activities.

**Start of Insurgency**

By the '60s-'70s various Meitei insurgent groups had formed, who demanded revival of the pre-Vaishnav Meitei culture and secession from India.

They agitated over:

- neglect,
- ceding of Kabaw Valley to Burma,
- granting only union territory status to Manipur when Nagaland had become a state,
- they had not been given scheduled tribe status whereas the hill tribes had,
- too much attention was being paid to the hill tribes who were getting preferential treatment in relation to the Meiteis simply because they had rebelled.

When counter-insurgency operations were launched by the Security Forces (SF), many groups moved out to the Chittagong Hill Tracts. Due to socio-economic deprivation, rising unemployment, and insurgency, the situation worsened. Politicians also started aligning themselves with various insurgent groups based on their ethnic consideration and sought for their support for elections and protection – political instability became the order of the day. This created an extremely complicated political situation and made governance very difficult. Some respite was obtained in the '70s as the 1971 war operations had terminated Pakistani support and there had been a series of successful counter-insurgency operations. However, increasing frustration, corrupt and poor governance, the continuing feud between the groups and subsequent support from Pakistan and Bangladesh resulted in a revival of insurgency by the '80–90s. To add to the complexities, the Pakistani and Bangladesh and reportedly the Chinese tried to get all the insurgent groups to join hands.

### NSCN (I&M) and Naga Kuki Strife

Most of the Naga insurgents in Manipur are led by Muivah's Tangkhuls in the NSCN (I&M)) which emerged from a split in the NSCN in '87–'88 and who have now more or less gained control of most Naga areas in Manipur and adjoining states. Besides secession and sovereignty, their demand is for merger of the Naga tribal areas of Manipur, Assam, Arunachal and Myanmar with Nagaland, which is one of the reasons for conflict with the Meiteis. Their conflict with the Kukis is for control over drug and other illegal trade traffic with Myanmar, besides the forcible interjection of the Kukis into traditional Naga areas.

Some of the Naga tribals, particularly those adjoining the Chakesang belt are part of the NFG (a derivative of the NNC), as this is an NFG stronghold opposed to the NSCN (I&M). Part of Tamenglong district in west Manipur continues to support the NSCN (K)

### Meitei – Kuki Conflict

The Meitei – Kuki conflict is based on a number of factors such as:

- forcible occupation of Meitei areas by the Kukis-Chins-Mizos,
- demand of Kuki-Chin tribes for Greater Mizoram, encompassing all areas occupied by their ethnic groups in Manipur, south Assam and Chin Hills,
- control over illegal trade in south Manipur.

The Kukis-Chin-Mizo tribals have been alienated on the grounds that since the British settled them in these areas, it was the duty of the

Indian government to protect them. Being from the same ethnic group as the Mizos of Mizoram, and with a demand for a merger of all Kukis-Chin-Mizo areas in Manipur with Mizoram, they supported the Mizo insurgency in the '60s-'70s. In the '80s and '90s, the Meiteis and then the Nagas engaged in trying to throw out the Kuki-Chin-Mizo tribals from the areas occupied by them and killed a large number of them. They now have fortified themselves into organised insurgent groups, whose role is to strike back at depredations against them by the Nagas and the Meiteis and their own sub-groups, and to try to achieve amalgamation of their areas with Mizoram and Chin Hills.

### *NSCN (I&M) – Kuki Alliance*
There is now reportedly a truce between some of the Kuki-Chin groups and NSCN (I&M) (a temporary marriage of convenience) and they have joined forces against the Meiteis with the NSCN promising them Greater Mizoram when Greater Nagaland comes through. As part of this strategy, NSCN (I&M) and allied Kuki-Chins groups are trying to strangle the Meiteis into submission, as they jointly control routes through the hills leading into Manipur. The recent blockade by the hill tribes of all routes leading into Manipur periodically for fairly long durations is part of their strategy.

### *NSCN (I&M) Ceasefire*
After the NSCN (I&M) ceasefire came into vogue, it applied only to the state of Nagaland. NSCN's attempt was to get it extended to cover the entire NSCN (I&M) – claimed areas, which included almost the whole of Manipur, major parts of south Assam and Tirap, Changlang and Lohit Districts of Arunachal, so they could gain control of the area during the ceasefire, notwithstanding the rivalry of some Naga tribes with the Tangkhuls. Delhi initially gave their approval to this proposal of NSCN (I&M). This led to extremely widespread agitation and strife by the Meiteis – Delhi was then forced to officially retract its earlier decision. There is however an unofficial ceasefire in the claimed areas of NSCN (I&M), between the NSCN (I&M) and their surrogate groups and the security forces, apparently out of fear that talks with the authorities will otherwise break down. Consequently, the NSCN (I&M) have had a free run in the claimed areas, much to the chagrin of the Meiteis, the Kuki-Chins, the residents of these areas and the state governments.

### Reaction of Meiteis to Unofficial Ceasefire

As a result of intense counter insurgency operations in Manipur against various insurgent groups, to try and bring the situation under control, many insurgent groups have shifted their sanctuaries to Myanmar, Bangladesh and adjoining states. Since the counter-insurgency operations are currently only against insurgent groups who are not party to the ceasefire – primarily the Meiteis – they are aggrieved. This, coupled with the actions of the hill tribes (who occupy the hills surrounding the Meitei areas of habitation on the valley floor), in trying to strangle the Meiteis into submission by frequent blockade of all roads leading into Manipur for long periods; the Meiteis find their backs to the wall and are becoming more alienated. This is even more so on account of the fact that the Meitei population at large has repeatedly proved their loyalty by fielding maximum people from the north-east in the national sports teams, the bureaucracy, police, armed forces and other central services.

The Meitei insurgent elements, which are visible, have in retaliation therefore launched a sustained campaign to malign the Indian government, the SF, the Armed Forces Special Powers Act, for violation of human rights. Their aim is to try and get the SF removed from Manipur, with a view to fight it out with the hill tribes on their own. I propose to cover matters related to such a step in a subsequent chapter, as the repercussions of this are likely to be extremely complex and grave. There is also a strong nexus between the insurgents and politicians; the deep-seated political instability in the state is a fall-out of the insurgents dictating terms to willing politicians. Further, as the political majority is Meitei, due to inter-ethnic animosity, there is a lack of development in the hill districts and a great deal of social deprivation particularly amongst the hill tribes. This only contributes further to the ethnic divide. The overall lack of law and order in the state has spawned extensive extortion by all the insurgent groups.

### Summation of Manipur's Problems:
- its political boundaries,
- sponsored migration of the Kuki-Chin tribes into traditional Naga and Meitei areas,
- creation of Nagaland and Mizoram and exclusion of the Naga and Kuki-Chin tribes in Manipur from them,
- Meitei perception that the Naga and Kuki-Chin tribes are perpetually being given favoured treatment whereas their interests have been neglected,

- continued bad and corrupt governance and the nexus between the state machinery and the insurgents,
- parcelling out Meitei territory to Myanmar,
- feuds between, the Meitei – Naga tribes, Meitei-Kuki-Chin tribes, Naga-Kuki-Chin tribes, hill versus valley dwellers; and as a recent addition, sub nationalism even within the sub tribes of the Kuki-Chin-Mizo group and feuds between them which are exploited by both the NSCN and the Meiteis,
- perception of the hill tribes that they have been totally neglected by the Meitei majority,
- demands of the Nagas and the Kuki-Chins for amalgamation into Greater Nagaland and Mizoram respectively and staunch Meitei resistance to the same,
- Meiteis feeling totally beleaguered and hemmed in by the hill tribes who control all entry and exit points into Manipur,
- the ceasefire and talks with NSCN (I&M) and the perceived favouritism shown to them by the Indian government,
- battle between a multitude of insurgent parties who support their respective ethnic groups,
- feuds between the above groups, and the security forces to gain control over areas of economic advantage and the drug/arms/timber/Chinese goods smuggling trade,
- indulgence by the rebels in large-scale extortion, intimidation and crime,
- economic and developmental retardation in the entire state.

**Comment**

In a nutshell, the situation in Manipur critical – much worse than Jammu and Kashmir and it is deteriorating further due to apathy and mismanagement. I would strongly urge those involved in the peace process with the NSCN (I&M) and policy making, to take heed of all these facts, when trying to break a deal.

There is an urgent need to resolve the problems in this region in a comprehensive fashion, after due deliberation and forethought, whilst ensuring a fair deal to all concerned ethnic groups – but speedily, if the situation is to be brought under control.

# 5
# MEGHALAYA, MIZORAM AND TRIPURA

## MEGHALAYA

### Demography

Meghalaya is a hill state with Assam to its north and east and Bangladesh to its south and west. Its population is 23,06,069 as per the 2001 census.

Its demographic profile is:

- Khasis/Jaintias/Garos 68%,
- Dimasa/Hmar/Kuki/Karbi/Lakher/Hajong/Mon/Naga 10%,
- Mizo 4%,
- Others (including Bangladeshi and Nepalese migrants) about 18%.

The Khasis, Jaintias and the Karbis are of Austric origin whereas the Garos, Dimasa and Hajongs are of Bodo origin.

### History

Historically, Meghalaya was excluded from the Mughal, Ahom and Burmese invasions on account of its inaccessibility. The British annexed it in 1835 and decided to set up their headquarters at Shillong, the capital of Meghalaya, for control of the north-east (undivided Assam), on account of its salubrious climate and relatively easier access. They therefore set up a more effective administration, while allowing limited autonomy. This area was not therefore given a segregated 'Excluded Area' status as was done for Nagaland and Mizoram and was amalgamated into the Assam administration. The British set about civilising the tribals through conversion to Christianity. As they were not segregated and there was greater interaction with other communities unlike the other hill states, they progressively accepted their merger with the Indian Union more gracefully, whilst maintaining their culture modified by Christian and western influence.

**Political Awakening**
Independence brought political awakening; demands for a separate state started from 1949. In 1952 the Khasis and Mizos led the demand for a separate tribal identity as they felt the Assam government was neglecting them. Demands for throwing out non-tribals started in 1957, particularly after observing the demographic changes in Tripura (Tripura earlier had a tribal majority, but due to excessive migration, the tribals became a minority) and Assam (the Assamese were progressively getting overwhelmed by Bangladeshi migration). Perceived social deprivation led to frustration and agitation against the Assam government. Seeing the Naga example, the youth began to agitate for insurrection to enforce their demands. Delhi decided to grant them statehood in 1972, thereby partially resolving the problem. A glance at the state's demographic profile however clearly indicates that the state also has a problem of Bangladeshi and Nepalese migration – the tribals therefore from fear initiated a movement against non-tribals, migrated into Meghalaya in large numbers, which continues till date. There are also issues of economic disparity due to lack of development – the Khasis feel that areas where there has been rebellion are much better-off as the centre has poured in resources for development into those areas.

**The Present Situation**
Today Meghalaya has a nascent Khasi/Jaintia insurgent movement organised into the Hynniewtrep National Liberation Council (HNLC) and Achik National Volunteer Council (ANVC) (Garo), with ULFA, NSCN (I&M), NDFB, Bangladeshi and Pakistani support, which propagate secession and an anti-migrant philosophy. Whereas previously the anti-migrant philosophy was primarily one of targeting the Bengalis and Nepalese, today the Khasis have also started targeting all other communities including tribals from other north-east states. There is also alienation between the Khasis and the Garos/Bodo tribals on ethnic grounds and talk of splitting the state further. In the late '90s and early 21$^{st}$ century the situation in Meghalaya had turned bad with extensive extortion being the order of the day. Consequently a very large number of outsiders who were involved in business and trade

fled the state. Fortunately the police have largely regained control and are now relatively more effective in keeping law and order under control. The anti-migrant and politically-sponsored Khasi-Garo agitations however continue unabated with frequent strikes and curfews consequent to which the state is unable to function effectively.

Meghalaya is well-endowed with natural resources, but has little industrial development. Consequently, its economic situation is poor. In a nutshell, the problem is socio-economic and coloured by ethnic strife and nascent insurgency which needs to be resolved by good governance.

## MIZORAM

### Demography

Mizoram is hilly, with a mean altitude ranging between 3000–4000 feet. It has Manipur and Assam to its north, Tripura and Bangladesh to its west, Myanmar to its east and Bangladesh to its south. Its 2001 census population is 8,91,058.

The demographic profile is:

- Mizos (Lushai) 60%,
- Paite 5%,
- Hmar 5%,
- Riang 5%,
- Poi 5%,
- Lakher/Pawi 8%,
- Chakma 7%,
- Others including Bangladeshi and Myanmar migrants 5%.

Mizoram has a demographic advantage over other north-eastern states – it is relatively homogenous (75% of its people are anthropologically from the Kuki-Chin-Mizo group of tribes) with adjoining areas of Myanmar (Chin Hills), south Manipur, south-eastern Tripura, and adjoining areas of Assam having similar Kuki-Chin-Mizo ethnic profiles.

### History

The Mizos were distinctive, fierce and warring, who started migrating from the Chin Hills in Myanmar into the Mizo Hills around the 11th century. The Bodos, Manipuris and the British permitted them autonomy as it was too expensive to subjugate them. It was only after the Mizos repeatedly raided British colonies and plantations in the late 19th century that the British launched a major expedition against them, subjugated them and colonised Mizo Hills. Even after doing so the British allowed them autonomy in all tribal affairs as they had done in the case of the Nagas. Administration of the Mizo Hills was comparatively simpler as the Mizo people were largely homogenous and less exposed to politics of the region. Here also the British segregated them from the plains through promulgation of the 'Inner Line' and encouraged conversion to Christianity. Like the Nagas and other isolated tribes, prior to conversion to Christianity, the religion was animism and their beliefs based on the primordial value system of 'tribe – village – land – autonomy'. Conversion to Christianity, accompanying westernisation and literacy has not changed this substantially. It is due to this that there is animosity towards other tribes and communities of the north-east particularly against the plains. It is also due to these ethnic considerations that part of the demand of the Mizos has always been for a Greater Mizoram encompassing the Chin Hills in Myanmar, parts of south Assam, south Tripura and south Manipur. It is also due to these considerations that Mizoram still has some problems with its minorities which are explained subsequently.

**Political Awakening**
Political groupings commenced just prior to partition – with demands being made initially for autonomy which changed to secession and independence to form Greater Mizoram – that subsequently after a long period of insurgency, changed to incorporation into the Indian Union, subject to grant of greater autonomy. Unfortunately, due to faulty policy after Indian independence, the British policy of segregation through the Inner Line restrictions was continued, with governmental neglect, lack of development, mal-administration and imposition of Assamese as the state language, leading to discontent and alienation. There were major famine conditions in Mizoram from 1959 to 1961 – during this period the people witnessed mismanagement and lack of assistance by the government – this resulted in isolation and formation of the Mizo National Front in 1961. After building up a support base amongst the people and taking cue from Nagaland and Manipur, the MNF declared Mizoram independent unilaterally in 1966 and commenced insurrection. They received support from Pakistan, China

and people from the Kuki – Chin group of tribes in neighbouring areas.

Counter-insurgency operations were launched immediately in 1966 to bring the situation under control. These were particularly successful after Pakistan was defeated in the 1971 war. Mizoram was then declared a 'union territory' and elections were held. With a political process having been initiated, the MNF progressively lost popular support. Talks were then initiated with the insurgents. Insurgency stepped up again after Bangladesh came under military rule with operations dragging till 1987. The operations culminated in the Mizo Accord, with insurgents coming over-ground and surrendering their arms, accepting the Indian Constitution, forming government, accepting grant of statehood and bringing peace to Mizo Hills. The provisions of the Accord also catered for autonomy in tribal affairs, rehabilitation of surrendered militants and examination of the feasibility of Greater Mizoram within the ambit of the Indian constitution.

**The Present Situation**
Since then Mizoram has progressed by leaps and bounds and is the second most peaceful state in the north-east (Sikkim being the most peaceful). Mizoram does however have:

- Problems related to its minorities i.e. the Hmars, Paites, Riangs (Brus), Pois, Lakhers, Chakmas and illegal immigration of Bangladeshi and Myanmar inhabitants. It has partially resolved the problem by grant of limited autonomy to some of the minorities. Some others have been coerced into an exodus out of the state into Tripura – particularly the Reangs and Chakmas, which is adversely affecting the already delicate situation in that state.
- Periodic demands of 'Greater Mizoram' for which some of its people, including those in authority, assist insurgents of the Kuki-Chin-Mizo ethnic group, in neighbouring Myanmar (Chin Hills) and south Manipur.
- It is also supportive of the NSCN (I&M) – at least conceptually, as some of those currently in power are close to them.
- It is opposed to migration from Bangladesh and is largely antagonistic towards it.
- All these aspects have resulted in strained relations with the neighbouring states/country.

- It is also over-urbanised (almost 60% of its population are dwellers of urban areas). This happened as groupings of villages were made on the Malaysian model, as part of counter-insurgency operations in the late '60s. With the grant of statehood and sudden large-scale employment avenues in the government, migration to urban areas increased substantially. In consequence, large urban areas have developed with multi-storied concrete constructions in earthquake-prone zones which are subject to frequent landslides. The urban areas have acute problems of availability of infrastructure in terms of water-supply, sanitation, roads and so on.
- Urbanisation has also led to neglect of the agricultural sector with consequent serious adverse effects.
- There is very little industrialisation.
- Mizoram, by virtue of its geographic location and peaceful situation with little or no security force deployment, is also an infiltration route for militants of all hues transiting to and from both Bangladesh and Myanmar militant sanctuaries. There is also arms and drug-smuggling into the region again from both these two countries. (Most of the arms-smuggling into the north-east is by ship from either Pakistan or South-East Asia into Cox Bazaar in Bangladesh and from there and Mizoram into Myanmar, Manipur and Assam.) Myanmar is a major drug-producing region and on the UN Narcotics watch-list.

## TRIPURA

### Demography

Tripura is a state with an ancient history. Its eastern and south-eastern parts are covered with low hills, which taper out into the plains of central and northern Tripura. It has Assam to its north, Mizoram and Manipur to its east and Bangladesh to its south and west. Its 2001 census population is 31,91,168.

Its demographic profile is:

- Tripuri tribes (Bodo origin) 15%,
- Riangs (Brus) 4%,
- Jamatias – Garos (Bodo origin) – Chakmas – Mizos – Kukis – Austrics 9%,

- Bengali Hindus 63%,
- Bengali Muslims 8%,
- Others 1%.

Presently tribal people reside primarily in the hill regions, with the plains populated by Bengalis.

## History

The predominant tribes were of Bodo origin called Tripuris, who established a kingdom in the middle ages consisting of the Arakan, Chittagong Hill Tracts, western Bangladesh, south Assam and present-day Tripura. Till the middle ages, they were a power centre in the region. The population till 1921 was tribal predominant, however consequent to British policy of encouraging immigration from East Bengal to under populated areas, there was extensive migration which continued till well after the Partition, Independence and then again in 1971, due to which tribal percentage reduced to about 28%. The Chakmas (4–5%) and Riangs (4%) are mainly recent immigrants, who fled from Chittagong Hill tracts and Mizoram following agitation and rebellion by them against the Bangladesh and Mizoram governments and the consequent clamp-down on them when they agitated for better socio-economic conditions.

## Insurgency

The state is beset by insurgency, by tribals of Bodo origin against the non-tribals. The key factors for the insurgency are overwhelming demographic change which threaten to wipe out the tribals and their distinctive culture, dislocation of the tribals from their traditional habitats and socio-economic deprivation. The insurgency, which is essentially rural, is aided and abetted by Pakistan and Bangladesh, and aimed at trying to throw out the migrants who now rule them and has continued on and off since 1949. Unfortunately, immigration has continued, though at a lower scale. The Army has had to be called out frequently to bring the situation under control. Though there have been peace talks and agreements in the past, they have fallen through due to demands not having been met and political parties siding various insurgent groups and use of the insurgents for political ends. The state is also a major infiltration route for insurgents transiting to and from Bangladesh and gun running. A large number of Security Forces are deployed both for border sealing and counter insurgency operations in the state.

**Economic Issues**
While the state is relatively rich in natural resources – particularly natural gas, and rubber, it has very little industry and is relatively underdeveloped. Tripura and Mizoram's geographic location and India's strained relations with Bangladesh create acute economic problems, as these states are out on a limb for surface communications with the rest of India after partition. Rationally, all transit goods should have been through Bangladesh to West Bengal or to Chittagong port and onwards. Alternatively, such an arrangement is needed with Myanmar to the Arakan coast. However, due to lack of such an agreement with Bangladesh or Myanmar, this is limited to movement by air only. Though this is cheaper for normal travel than surface communications, it is uneconomical for bulk trade. The two states therefore suffer from acute economic problems and lack of development. It is imperative that Delhi resolves with Bangladesh the issues of transit trade, Bangladeshi support to the insurgents and that Tripura resolves its problems related to the tribals through a series of measures, which are discussed in subsequent chapters.

# 6
# ARUNACHAL, SIKKIM AND NORTH BENGAL

## ARUNACHAL

### Demography

Arunachal Pradesh is the largest and least developed hill state of the region. It covers the mountain ranges of the eastern Himalayas and is located to the north, east and south-east of Assam. Its neighbours besides Assam include Tibet (China) to its north and east, Myanmar to its east, Bhutan to its west and Nagaland to its south-west. Its 2001 census population is 10,91,117.

It has well over 100 ethnic groups of which 20 are considered to be major tribes. The demographic profile of its 20 main tribes is:

- Adis (Padam, Minyong, Pasi, Pangi etc) 27%, (inhabitants of Siang and Dibang)
- Nissi/Dafla 22%, (inhabitants of Subansiri and South Kameng)
- Wangchoos 8%, (inhabitants of Tirap ethnic lineage akin to Nagas)
- Monpa 8%, (inhabitants of North Kameng and a few other areas on Tibet border)
- Mishmi 7%, (inhabitants of Lohit lineage probably a mix of Bodo and Naga
- Nocte 7%, (inhabitants of Lohit lineage somewhat akin to Nagas)
- Tagins 6%, (inhabitants of South Kameng and parts of Subansiri)
- Tangsas 4%, (inhabitants of Lohit )
- Apatani 4%, (inhabitants of Subansiri)
- Miris 2%, (inhabitants of Northern Foothills of Brahmaputra valley)
- Sulungs 1%. (again inhabitants of the foothills)
- Khamptis 1%, (inhabitants of Changlang Lineage a mix of Naga and Bodo)

- Others (includes migrant Chakmas, Tibetans, Nepalese, Bangladeshis) 3–4%. (Tibetan refugees who fled on Chinese occupation of Tibet and Chakma migrants who fled Bangladesh have been settled on the plains of Lohit and Changlang. There is a fairly large Nepalese colony in a remote area bordering Myanmar. These people are descendants of Assam Rifles personnel who have border-guarding posts in the area. There is also a fair sprinkling of Nepalese spread all along the southern fringes of the state near areas where the Assam Rifles had established themselves during British rule. Bangladeshi migrants have again settled along the southern fringes of the state in the Brahmaputra valley.)

A clear ethnic division is also discernable on account the population being split into four distinct lineages:

- Tibetan (Monpas/Tibetans),
- Indo-Burmese (including those with affinity to the Naga tribes) (Wangchoos, Mishmi, Tangsas, Khamptis, Noctes)
- Bodo origin (the other tribes)
- Others – migrants who have settled in Arunachal

The people, with such a multitude of diverse ethnic formations, have an extremely rich cultural heritage. The majority of people particularly in the remoter areas are all animists with primordial beliefs. The first missionaries into Arunachal were the Rama Krishna Missions, who are well-liked for their efforts in the social field. Due to their missionary efforts, Arunachal today has a fair number of followers of the Hindu faith particularly in the southern belt of north Arunachal. The tribes of Tibetan origin are all Budhists. Christianity is also picking up particularly in the districts of Tirap, Changlang and Lohit due to the efforts of the NSCN. Arunachal is one part of India where one can find areas almost untouched by civilisation with natural pristine beauty and a population that still totally believes in its primordial value system of 'tribe – village – land autonomy' and makes concerted efforts to protect the same.

## History

Arunachal is the most diverse and yet peaceful state – primarily due to its small population being interspersed in a huge and relatively inaccessible area, being heavily forested, under-developed with few roads, thereby ensuring relative isolation and distinctiveness for its diverse ethnic groups in most interior areas. It is also due to these reasons that the political reach of the state to these areas is limited thereby ensuring a great deal of autonomy. It is also the most recent state to be opened up to administration. It was only in 1882 that exploration and subjugation by the British began, consequent to the British adopting a forward policy of defending its frontiers with reference to Russia and China (for fear of either of these powers posing a threat to Imperial India – in fact time has proved the British apprehensions to be correct).

Prior to British times the Bodos and Ahoms left the Arunachal tribes well alone and allowed them autonomy. The British had named the area the North East Frontier Tracts and by 1914, attempted to administer it through the North East Frontier Tracts administration, with near total autonomy in all tribal matters. The Inner Line Regulation was also invoked and the region was given 'Excluded Area' status. This implied that no non-residents were permitted to enter the area without permission. The British (purportedly to prevent exploitation by the plains people and traders) did this; in fact, this was done to isolate the hill tribes from the politics of the 'Free India' movement that was sweeping across India. As the area was totally segregated and largely unexplored, it remained unaffected by politics. After Independence, India continued with the British policy. In 1954, the area was renamed North East Frontier Agency (NEFA) and due to the border dispute with China, the Army and Assam Rifles moved in. In 1957, due to the Naga insurgency, Tuensang Frontier Division adjoining Nagaland and Myanmar Naga Hills with a primarily Konyak Naga tribal population, was merged with the Naga Hills.

## The Indo-China Boundary Dispute

The Chinese, from the mid '50s onwards have laid claim to the entire area of Arunachal Pradesh north of the River Lohit which borders Tibet, on grounds that this entire area was directly under Tibetan suzerainty and administration prior to the forcible occupation of the area by the British. The British are also blamed for drawing up a false and illegal boundary between India and Tibet called the 'Macmohan Line' and forcing the Tibetans to accept it in 1914 – this boundary is considered unacceptable by the Chinese. After the boundary dispute became evident in the late '50s and Tibet was occupied by Chinese troops, Indian forces were moved into this area upto the perceived alignment of the Macmohan Line. This led to confrontation between the Chinese and Indian forces and ultimately the 1962 Indo-China conflict. Due to being ill prepared, India suffered a humiliating defeat.

Since then the Indian Army has taken adequate measures to ensure that such an event is never repeated. The entire border belt is under occupation by Indian Forces with Chinese forces deployed opposite. A Border Peace and Tranquillity Accord is in place between the two countries since the '90s, wherein it has been agreed that all disputes will be resolved through talks and a number of confidence building measures have since been instituted. Talks between India and China are in progress to try and resolve the boundary question – however as the issues involved are complex and there is also a great deal of distrust for each other after so many years of animosity, I have no doubt in my mind that the dispute may take quite some time to resolve. India had however in the course of these events seen the need to bring the area under more effective administrative control due to Chinese claims to the area. Hence the 'Panchayat system' was introduced in 1967. In 1972, Arunachal Pradesh became a union territory and in 1987 it was granted full statehood.

**Economy**

The economy is largely agricultural, which is the mainstay of its people. It has tremendous forest wealth and in all probability extensive mineral deposits which have not yet been exploited. It also has great potential in the field of hydroelectric power – again yet to be exploited – though it is understood that measures are in hand to do so in the main river valleys starting with the Subansiri River Valley. Once this is done Arunachal will be able to supplement its income substantially through sale of power to Assam and possibly north Nagaland. A certain amount of attention is also now being paid to commercial exploitation of handicrafts, which are diverse and plentiful in the state.

**Key Problem Areas**

Its main problems are:

- the border disputes, with China still claiming the whole of Arunachal bordering Tibet, which has been discussed above;
- threat of change of demographic profile, due to resettlement of Chakmas and Tibetans in the state on instructions of the central government and the migration of Bangladeshis and Nepalese; it needs to be understood that as the resettlement and maximum

migration is into Lohit and Changlang districts, it is the ethnic groups inhabiting these areas that fear demographic change and are agitating against the same;
- lack of economic development and therefore socio economic deprivation and consequent ethnic rivalry; and claims to Lohit, Tirap and Changlang districts of the state by the Nagas. As the Adis and the Nissis form the majority population in Arunachal, the minority groups complain of discrimination and neglect particularly in the districts of Tirap, Changlang and Lohit which are claimed by the Nagas. There have been budding insurgent groups that keep emerging particularly from these minority districts, linked to the NSCN, which need to be continuously nipped in the bud.
- Tirap, Changlang and part of Lohit districts are affected by both the Naga and the Assam insurgency – with the NSCN (I&M) claiming all three districts right up to the Tibetan border as part of Greater Nagaland and the area being a battle ground between the NSCN (I&M) and the NSCN (K) for control of the area. The ULFA is using the area for sanctuary and transit to their camps in Myanmar. The state is against a merger of these claimed areas with Nagaland, or for its territory to be used by any of the insurgent groups. Counter insurgency operations by security forces are therefore being conducted against these insurgent groups in the affected areas.

The main issue in the state that needs to be attended to is the requirement for better governance which would meet the aspirations of the minorities.

## SIKKIM

### Demography

Sikkim is the most peaceful state of the region. It is lies in the eastern Himalayas, with Tibet (China) to its north, Bhutan to its east, West Bengal to its south and Nepal to its west. It has the least population amongst all the states in the country – 5,40,493. Its demographic profile is:

- Nepalese 80%,
- Lepchas and Bhutias 19%,
- Others 1%.

## History

The state has no documented history earlier than the 17th century. However, classical and religious literature, folklore, legends and anthropological findings indicate that the earliest inhabitants were Austrics, who were overwhelmed by the migratory hordes of the Bodo tribes in both southern Tibet and present-day Sikkim, well before the birth of Christ. Legends and folklore indicate the Lepchas (Bodo origin) migrating into Chumbi Valley (now part of Tibet and then part of Sikkim) and establishing a kingdom encompassing the Chumbi Valley, present-day Sikkim and Darjeeling district of North Bengal. During the middle ages there were Tibetan migrations (again of Bodo origin called Bhutias) into Sikkim. After settling in Sikkim the Bhutias joined hands with the Lepchas within a period of time and formed a dynasty headed by the Chogyal that ruled Sikkim till 1975, when it merged with India consequent to political awakening and demands for democracy.

In the 18th century, Nepal tried to colonise Sikkim and parts of southern Tibet, which resulted in British assistance being sought and the Nepalese and Tibetans defeated. This led to Sikkim, Bhutan and Tibet being given a 'Protectorate' status and Chumbi Valley being ceded to Tibet. The British established their base in Darjeeling district of North Bengal, to control North Bengal, eastern Nepal, Sikkim and western Bhutan and demanded that Darjeeling district be leased to them – Sikkim duly complied. The large Nepalese migration was mainly during this period. After Independence, India continued with the British Protectorate status till Sikkim merged with India. The border dispute with China wherein the Chinese recognised an independent Sikkim, but not its initial 'Protectorate' status and subsequent merger with India, led to large-scale induction of Indian troops into Sikkim in the late '50s and Chinese troops into Chumbi Valley and their being deployed opposite each other almost eyeball to eyeball. This Army presence from both sides, though at a reduced scale, continues till date.

## The Present Situation

As the state is peaceful, it has emerged as a major national and international tourist destination – this is the mainstay of the state's economy. Due to small size of the population, tourism, mining and handicraft incomes, central government assistance, extensive infrastructure development consequent to Army deployment over the past 40 odd years and with relatively good governance the state is economically the best-off in the region. The likelihood of trade opening up through Sikkim with China has also improved its prospects. There has been little cause for unrest in the state too.

**Key Problem Areas**
Notwithstanding the above, there are reports of western Sikkim and Darjeeling district, being used as sanctuary for the 'Maoists' (Left Extremists) of both India and Nepal and some other Indian insurgent groups including the ULFA, KLO, NDFB, and even the NSCN. There are also periodic reports about Nepalese/Gurkha hardliners amongst the Maoists, with demands for a united Gurkhaland consisting of Nepal, Sikkim, Darjeeling and parts of Jalpaiguri district of North Bengal and parts of southern Bhutan, which are causes of concern and need to be monitored and suitably addressed.

## NORTH BENGAL

**Demography**
North Bengal consists of Jalpaiguri, Darjeeling, Cooch Behar and North Dinajpur districts of North Bengal. The area has a population of approximately 9.4 million with a multitude of ethnic formations. Though the detailed demographic profile is not available, it includes:

- Domicile Bengalis (the majority),
- Bangladeshi migrants (very substantial numbers),
- Biharis,
- Gurkhas,
- Bodo origin groups, including Rajbangshis – Koches (who prefer being called Kamtapuris),
- Assamese,
- Tea Tribes (from Chota Nagpur Plateau),
- Bhutias and others (from all over India).

**History**
The ancient history of the region is not documented enough. Folklore, the epics and scientific evidence indicate the original inhabitants to have been Austrics, who were overwhelmed by mongoloid (Bodo group of tribes) migrations well before the birth of Christ. The epics indicate it to have been part of the Bodo Kingdom of Kamrupa also in the pre-Christian era. The western parts were overrun and formed part

of the Gupta and then Mauryan dynasties. From the 4$^{th}$/5$^{th}$ century onwards, western parts were ruled by the Pala and then Sena dynasties of Bengal – however the eastern parts (Cooch Behar and part of Jalpaiguri) were ruled by dynasties of Bodo origin tempered with Aryan inter-mixing – Kamtapuris. In the medieval period, the Muslim Sultanate and subsequently the Mughals conquered and ruled the area, excluding Darjeeling and Cooch Behar. The advent of the British resulted in annexation of the entire area except Cooch Behar, which became a princely state allied to the British. Darjeeling district became the British administrative base in North Bengal for control of the entire surrounding area. Consequent to Independence and merger of Cooch Behar with India, the entire area including Darjeeling district became part of West Bengal.

**Migration**
The migration of Nepalese, Bangladeshis, Tea tribes, Biharis and many others commenced from the 18$^{th}$ century onwards in conformity with British policy to populate and develop the area like in Assam. The migrations continued with Partition, Independence and then again in 1971. Afterwards, it has continued at a much slower pace. It is due to the migrations that there has been demographic changes responsible for greater pressure on the land, with consequent socio-economic deprivation and a major cause for discontent, as was witnessed from the Naxalite activities of the late '60s, early '70s, the recent revival of the Left and GNLF movements and the current Kamtapuri Liberation Organisation (KLO) as well as the Maoist activities.

**Key Problem Areas**
North Bengal has a number of major problem areas, which need to be addressed.

- Firstly, the discontent of the tribals consequent to the demographic change and a feeling of neglect, particularly amongst those of Bodo origin, has led to the nascent KLO insurgency, with demands for a separate state. The KLO has allied itself to the ULFA and the Maoists and has Bangladeshi support.
- Discontent amongst the Gurkhas/Nepalese in Darjeeling (the GNLF and allied groups) and Gurkha populated areas of Jalpaiguri over issues of neglect and socio-economic deprivation and their consequent demands for autonomy. This discontent,

when considered in conjunction with the developing link-up between the more extreme elements of the GNLF and the Maoists of Nepal, Bengal and Bihar, which are growing surely but steadily, are dangerous portends and indicate a distinct possibility of insurgency breaking out.
- Demographic change that has taken place in North Bengal has resulted in certain pockets becoming vulnerable to religious fundamentalist group activities.
- The region is being used as sanctuary for other north-east insurgent groups and the Maoists. When considered along with the relatively lower level of development and economic activity, it is indeed a very unhealthy trend, coupled with the left extremism that is steadily taking root.
- When considered collectively and along with the fact that this area (the Siliguri Corridor) is India's lifeline to the north-east, the situation is literally like a time bomb, which if not diffused immediately, may explode with disastrous consequences. All this has occurred due to the inadequacies in governance – the existing authorities would do well to do some introspection and rectify the situation. It has occurred due to complacency and callousness in attitudes of the ruling parties.

There is also an urgent requirement to develop the area and improve its economy so that it becomes capable of acting as a commercial centre for surface communications and trade for the entire north-east and with China. If this is done diligently, it will automatically resolve many of the region's intrinsic problems.

# 7
# ROLE OF SERVICEMEN & EX-SERVICEMEN IN THE REGION

In the preceding chapters, we had an overview of the region and all the states, including major problem areas that need to be addressed. In this chapter, I will familiarise the readers with certain little-known facts related to the role of servicemen (SM) and ex-servicemen (ESM) of the armed forces, Para Military Forces (PMF) and Central Police Organisations (CPOs) in nation-building in their respective regions.

## DEMOGRAPHY OF SERVICEMEN/EX-SERVICEMEN

**Ukhrul District of Manipur**
This district, the heartland of the NSCN (I&M), has a 2001 census population of 1,40,000. Of this, about 7500 are ESM with another 500 SM from the Army. In addition, there are about 1000–1500 SM and ESM of the Assam Rifles and other PMF/CPOs, totalling to about 9000–10000. When one considers the SM/ESM as a family unit (father, mother, 3 or more children), we have a population of about 45,000 or about 30% of the total population of the district. All these are people for whom the parent organisations – the central and state governments – are duty-bound to look after and provide for in terms of pensions, healthcare, priority for education, canteen services, payment rations and for problem resolution. When one expands the family sizes to individuals that the SM/ESM can directly influence, i.e. his brothers and sisters and their children, the family unit size increases to about 10 or about 90,000 to 1 lakh – 65–70% of the total population of Ukhrul District.

Every village in the district has persons both serving and retired with many of the village headmen being ex-servicemen. The NSCN (I&M) have 2500–3000 men and women from the district. Whilst it is a confirmed fact that no SM/ESM are members of the insurgent group, it is also a fact that some of their relations are. This is on account of the fact that, the SM/ESM families are by far the worst off economically and socially and strongly feel that their parent organisations and governments have neglected them, in spite of their having given the best years in service of the nation. Their children feel this neglect particularly strongly, which prompts them to join the insurgents and pick up arms against the state.

### Rest of Manipur

Other hill districts of Manipur (Senapati, Tamenglong, Churachanpur and Chandel), which also contribute recruits from the families of SM/ESM to either the NSCN or the Kuki-Chin insurgent groups have similar percentages or even higher in some cases. They are comparatively worse off than Ukhrul due to the relative lack of ethnic homogeneity and a declining law and order situation.

The Meitei area also has a large percentage of SM/ESM including PMF/CPOs – about 15000–20000 or about 15% (as an expanded family unit). They again have similar grievances. Overall, as far as welfare of SM/ESM is concerned, Manipur is the most neglected and disorganised state in the north-east despite the fact that this state has the highest proportion of SM/ESM, both for reasons of the prevailing situation and lack of concern by those responsible. It does not even have functional 'Soldiers', Sailors' and Airmen's Boards' that are supposed to be set up by the state. In many cases, the ESM do not even get their pensions regularly.

### Nagaland

Nagaland has about 20,000 SM/ESM including PMF/CPOs, which constitute about 1% of its population, or 5% as a family unit which is about 12% as an expanded family unit. There are very few villages that do not have a representation, with quite a few ESM being village headmen. Here again, the refrain of the SM/ESM is the same – they feel neglected, though to a much lesser degree than Manipur (because of the recent interest taken by those in authority). Unlike Manipur however one does find very few relatives of SM/ESM in insurgent outfits, thanks to more stringent government checks.

### Mizoram

Mizoram has about 15,000 SM/ESM including CPOs/PMF, which constitute about 2% of the total population. As a basic family unit, it amounts to 75000 or about 10% and as an expanded family unit 1.5 lakhs or 20% of the total population. While welfare of SM/ESM is more organised in Mizoram – the situation of neglect still remains. This is account of the fact that those in authority, till recently, have had little sympathy for the ESM though the situation seems to have improved slightly.

## Assam
Assam has about 45,000 SM/ESM including CPOs/PMF or about 2% of its total population; about 10% when considered a family unit and 20% as considered to be an expanded family unit. As far as welfare of SM/ESM is concerned, things are disorganised with a complete lack of concern; the Rajya and other Sainik Boards are almost non-functional.

## Tripura
Tripura has only about 2500 SM/ESM. While there is not much being done for their welfare, they are a disorganised lot and have not demanded redress for their grievances in a cohesive manner.

## Arunachal
Arunachal again has only about 3000 SM/ESM. Even as an expanded family unit they form just about 2–3% of the total population – consequently there is a lack of awareness amongst them of their own welfare.

## Meghalaya
Meghalaya too has only small numbers of SM/ESM – about 3000, or about 2% when considered as an expanded family unit – here again there is a total lack of concern by the authorities and awareness amongst the local population.

## Sikkim
Sikkim also has a very small number – about 250 – less than 0.5% even as an expanded family unit – the lack of awareness and concern is evident.

## North Bengal
North Bengal has about 30,000 SM/ESM (about 3% only when considered as a family unit from complete North Bengal) – the majority of these personnel are Gurkhas from Darjeeling and Jalpaiguri districts,

where they form a much larger proportion – almost equating to the proportion in Assam, particularly in Darjeeling district. Here again, one sees lack of concern for their welfare and widespread neglect in spite of the GNLF movement having originated basically from the ESM group.

## Welfare of the ESM and Parent Organisations

The central government is responsible for the following ESM issues:

- remittance of pensions to the state government treasuries/ nominated nationalised banks,
- organising resettlement of ESM through training capsules and advice on their future,
- employment of some ESM in central government organisations and arranging employment for a limited number of ESM in trade,
- arranging loans for ESM self-employment schemes,
- certain actual welfare measures, including healthcare, education of their families in central government and armed forces institutions where available, rations on payment and canteen services through the defence services units where located close by.

The state governments are responsible for the following:

- ensuring correct and timely disbursement of pensions,
- organising resettlement including actual grass-root welfare through state and district level Sainik Boards,
- employment of ESM in state government services as per percentages laid down after mutual agreement between the two governments,
- arranging employment through locally based trade enterprises,
- arranging loans for self-employment schemes in consultation with the central government.

The armed forces through their local units are responsible for:

- implementing grass-root welfare measures wherever their units and formations are in proximity to ESM, including provision of healthcare through the ESM Health Scheme, issue of rations and canteen stores on payment, and resolution of problems where feasible,

- maintenance of liaison with the state governments to get problems of ESM resolved wherever the issues are beyond their purview.

## Reality and Actual Welfare

Unfortunately the parent organisations, including the armed forces are not located in all areas to handle these issues; also perhaps more importantly, all these organisations including the armed forces and their senior officers are too busy with the execution of their own duties to attend to this vital aspect. Most of the time, they are content with simply holding the ESM rally and neglect duties towards their welfare. The state governments, to a large extent, (except Nagaland which lately is putting in a concerted effort) do little or nothing, claiming lack of resources and even try to throw the ball back into the central government's court claiming that as the ESM retired from a central government organisation, they are the centre's headache. The central government in turn does precious little to either resolve these problems or try to improve the lot of the ESM – to the extent that they even fail to ensure that the state/central government machinery pays pensions regularly. They have also not ensured proper functioning of the armed forces agencies – even Soldiers', Sailors' and Airmen's boards are neither constituted nor functional in some states. Neither government has been able to institute suitable measures to restructure the existing system to make it effective.

## Role of ESM in Society

What role do the SM/ESM and their families play in society? These people, having retired early in life are still relatively young. They have lived all over the country in the most challenging circumstances, are well-disciplined, trained in a multitude of jobs and are good organisers and administrators. They are ideally suited to make their presence felt in society, if they are given suitable opportunity, which perhaps they ought to be given since they have sacrificed half their lives in defending their country. Leaving service amounts to a complete upheaval in lifestyle, acclimatisation to which can only be made easier with help from civil society.

In spite of the little or no help being given to them by their regional authorities, some of them are self-employed entrepreneurs, farmers, government employees, a few are in politics and some are heads in village *panchayats*. There are vast majorities of ESM however, particularly in the remote areas, who are very badly off and require assistance that is not forthcoming from any quarter.

## Remedial Measures Necessary

Steps that need to be taken to remedy the situation can be:

- The central government needs to initiate measures to restructure the existing pattern of welfare of separated SM families living in their villages and ESM and their families. For the interim, however, the existing system needs to be galvanised into functioning more effectively,
- The armed forces and Assam Rifles should take on welfare of families of the SM and ESM as a function of command and ensure they are proactive in this field as part of their civic action programs. Regiments that recruit troops from this region must put in much greater efforts towards welfare of the SM families and ESM.
- Rather than expecting doles, SM and ESM must band together to form co-operative business enterprises on a large scale, aimed at generating employment, income and therefore automatically welfare. These enterprises should be manned and run by the ESM and families of both SM and ESM, with the SM only offering advice and acting as checks on the system. The scope for doing so is enormous – it could be in the field of running transport services, construction, security services, agriculture as in co-operative farming, bamboo industry, herb culture, fish farming and export, production and export of handicrafts, tourism, horticulture, floriculture and so on. There may be problems of finding sufficient capital to start such enterprises – this could surely be resolved by grants/loans and organising things regimentally – each regiment of the Army could work out its own structure and a system of checks to prevent corruption and mismanagement. Such systems exist in many countries the world over including USA, Israel, Pakistan and China, where large business enterprises are both run and manned purely by ESM. Some efforts were made in this regard in the '60s in the form of Army Development Groups charged with the responsibility of creating infrastructure

and administration in border areas – it however died a natural death due to lack of interest from the government. Some officers have mooted such an idea for the north-east —unfortunately it is still to take off. This would ensure gainful employment for not only the ESM but also their families and counter the pressures that lead them to join insurgents.

# 8
# INDIA'S FOREIGN RELATIONS, THE EFFECT OF GEO-POWER POLITICS & EVENTS IN NEIGHBOURING COUNTRIES

In this chapter, I propose to give readers an overview of the effects of our foreign policy, power politics and events in the neighbouring countries, as they have had a profound effect on developments in the north-east.

**Effects of Partition of India**
The effects of the British policy of 'Divide and Rule' with reference to the Indian sub-continent's Hindus and Muslims are well-known and documented. Their consequent decision to partition the sub-continent into India, Pakistan and Myanmar and the way they drew up boundaries to do so, was perhaps one of the greatest blunders they committed throughout their colonial and imperial history. It resulted in anguish and massacres which had never been seen on the sub-continent, created millions of refugees fleeing to safety across artificially created boundaries, turmoil for people who had been split across these borders, and unrelenting hatred and distrust between India and Pakistan which continues till today. This is the backdrop to the foreign policies of both India and Pakistan since that fateful period of Partition and Independence.

The idea of creation of a homeland for the sub-continent's Muslims germinated in Bengal, arising out of the first Partition of Bengal by the British in 1919. After this, the so-called 'Muslim Homeland' was created through partition of the sub-continent by the British in 1947, in the form of East and West Pakistan. Whoever could have imagined that Pakistan would get balkanised in the fashion that occurred in 1971? It was the ethnic rivalry between the Punjabi and Bengali Muslims culminating in the crackdown by the Pakistani Army on the East Pakistani (Bengali) dissidents and Indian intervention that led to creation of Bangladesh in 1971. Creation of Bangladesh with Indian help, by no means changed the (East Pakistan's) original idea of it being a Muslim homeland. If anything it strengthened the determination of both Pakistan and Bangladesh to fulfil the idea and since the basic issue of ethnic autonomy between the two parts of Pakistan had been resolved, they decided to work together towards achieving this aim.

## Cause for Antagonism of Bangladesh and Pakistan

Partition was the result of communal disharmony and hatred fanned by those with vested interests. Creation of a Muslim homeland meant finding an identity and a place, which would not be cowed down by a huge 'Hindu India', irrespective of the fact that India's Muslims and other minorities outnumbered East and West Pakistan's population by almost 1.5:1. This complicated their identity crisis and coloured their views against India, the Hindu heartland and the common enemy. This is something most foreign and many Indian analysts fail to comprehend – the quarrel is NOT Kashmir – it is the issue of identity, coupled with Jammu and Kashmir, the north-east, Punjab, Gujarat, Rajasthan, Sindh, the Indus waters, maritime boundaries and so on. We consequently had the conflict of 1947–48 in Kashmir. Army rule in Pakistan from 1954 onwards and subsequently in Bangladesh, only strengthened their resolution to confront India at every cost.

## Effects of Dispute with China

The precipitating reasons for our dispute with China in the late '50s were:

- India assisted and gave sanctuary to Tibetan dissidents when the Chinese occupied Tibet;
- India reportedly allowed the United States to support Tibetan insurgents in Indian territory;
- China claimed parts of Indian territory along the border with Tibet and more particularly in the north-east, almost the whole of Arunachal and chunks of Bhutan who enjoyed India's protection.

The above resulted in China seizing the opportunity to support the

Naga insurgent movement and subsequently other north-east rebels and Left extremists in the manner they had earlier supported insurgencies the world over. India was unprepared for this *volte-face* and suffered a crushing defeat in 1962 from the Chinese. Pakistan immediately took advantage of our predicament, settled their purported border issue with China, befriended and allied with China. China from then on has used Pakistan to keep India in its place and to act as its proxy to aid insurgency in India, initially and primarily through East Pakistan for the north-east.

## Cold War and Annoyance of the West

We annoyed the West with our criticism of their policies and subsequently by seeking assistance of USSR during the Cold War – in their perception, we had joined the Eastern Bloc. Pakistan joined the Western Bloc – consequently aid flowed into Pakistan – which was used to fight the 1965 Indo-Pak war and fuel insurgency.

## Effect of China falling out with USSR

China had meanwhile fallen out with USSR on grounds of communist ideology. The Soviet Union communists were now of the view that socialism could be achieved through peaceful means. Maoist China on the other hand felt very strongly that this must be achieved only through an armed revolution or a People's War. They therefore broke away from the Soviet embrace and declared Soviet Union to be imperialist and an enemy. With our allying ourselves to USSR, India fell into the same category. Chinese antipathy towards India was compounded due to the border dispute and the war with their ally Pakistan in 1965. They therefore stepped up their support to India's north-east insurgents, adopted threatening postures along our northern borders and started wholehearted support to India's nascent Naxalite movement that was raging in Andhra, North Bengal and Orissa. Many analysts are of the view that the only reason for China not attacking India in 1965 was due to USSR's threat of intervention in India's favour. Post '65, the border skirmish with the Chinese in Sikkim resulted in continued aid to the Naga, Mizo and Manipuri insurgents flowing in through communist-controlled north Burma and East Pakistan. Also, due to Chinese support, the Naxalite movement spread to other parts of India including Assam and Tripura.

## 1971 War in the East

From the time of Pakistani independence, there was major ethnic rivalry between the Bengalis of East Pakistan and the Punjabis in West Pakistan over representation in the Pakistani government, economy and development. East Pakistani Bengalis felt they were not given their due in spite of their being more populous than West Pakistan and that a Punjabi minority was ruling them. The Bengalis also felt that they were not getting their due share of finance and for development. East Pakistan therefore tried to break away from Pakistan on ethnic grounds and started a freedom movement in the late '60s. This culminated in 1971 with the Pakistani Army taking repressive measures to quell the movement. There were tremendous atrocities against the Bengalis in East Pakistan, which resulted in very large-scale exodus of refugees into India. Pakistan accused India of supporting the movement and launched strikes against India along the western borders. This resulted in the 1971 war with Pakistan in which the USSR provided a shield against the Chinese and the US reportedly intervening in support of Pakistan. India fought a defensive battle in the west, while its armed forces, assisted by the Bangladeshi freedom fighters, fought in East Pakistan. In 14 days, the Pakistani Army in East Pakistan was defeated with almost 100,000 of its men surrendering to the Indian Armed Forces. East Pakistan was thus liberated from the West Pakistani yoke. It was probably the threat of US intervention that partly influenced the course of events and Bangladesh coming into being as an independent state.

## Effects of Pakistani Defeat

In the early '70s ambience of Pakistan's pre-occupation with the events of 1971, the Burmese reaching an understanding with China over activities in north Burma, initial Bangladeshi euphoria over Indian help, and ultimately the flurry of foreign policy activity in India to mend fences with the West and China, there was reduced support to the insurgents and Naxalites from both Pakistan and China. Consequently, and as a result of concerted and successful internal policies and counter-insurgency operations, the Naxalite problem was brought under control; a peace accord was reached with most of the Naga groups; Manipur and Mizoram were brought under control and the situation in the north-east improved. There was also a rapprochement between the US and China (Pakistan was allied to both) – who then joined hands to defeat USSR and its allies.

## Strategy of Proxy War

The Pakistani Army could NOT accept the disgrace of defeat, surrender and loss of power. They therefore seized power again after a short period of civilian rule and formulated a strategy of proxy war to try and defeat and balkanise India, with ideas borrowed from the Arabs in the Middle East (where a large proportion of the Pakistani Army and non-resident Pakistanis were serving at that time). They decided to make 'India bleed through a thousand cuts', by active support to all dissident movements and through religious fundamentalism and terrorism. They therefore converted Pakistan into an Islamic State. At the time of Independence, they had declared themselves to be a secular state due to having a fairly large number of religious minorities, but progressively drifted towards becoming Islamic. Pakistan realised that India could not be defeated through conventional war and therefore decided to "go nuclear" with well-equipped conventional forces, to deter India from retaliatory strikes. India, as a defence mechanism, was also then forced to adopt nuclear means. This annoyed both China and the West particularly since India was considered to be an ally of the USSR and this upset the cold war balance of power.

## Bangladesh Strategy

The Bangladesh Army, earlier part of the Pakistan Army, which had tasted power, took control of Bangladesh after the assassination of Sheikh Mujibur Rehman in 1975 through a coup. Both the armies joined hands to try and defeat India and achieve their original ideals. Bangladesh also continued with the pre-partition strategy of the Muslim League – to ensure maximum migration into the north-east and Bengal, so that after demographic change, these areas are seceded to Bangladesh. They knew that they could not defeat India conventionally – the strategy was therefore to ensure migration, ally with China and Pakistan, fan religious fundamentalism (they also converted into an Islamic State), build up conventional forces for defence and provide maximum support to Indian dissident groups.

## Start of the Proxy War and Chinese and Western Role

In 1978, Pakistan became the frontline state for the West and China to defeat USSR in Afghanistan – aid, weapons and funds poured in with much of it being used to achieve Pakistan's strategy. With commencement of the new strategy, Punjab burst into flames; training of Kashmiri dissidents and other religious fundamentalists commenced; NSCN emerged in Nagaland and Manipur as did other Manipuri dissident groups; the ULFA (Assamese) and NDFB (Bodo) insurgents were born; Mizoram and Tripura insurgency and left extremist groups were reactivated. By the early '80s, the north-east was in flames along with Punjab. Pakistani nuclear bomb preparations were also on at full blast. It is impossible that the West and China did not know about that, perhaps they even supported all these events, irrespective of claims to the contrary.

**Mending Fences**
The visit by our leaders to China in the early '80s and the change of guard in China resulted in reduced Chinese support to the north-east insurgents and possibly put pressure on Pakistan and Bangladesh to reduce their activities. Consequently the situation was brought under control in Punjab and the Mizo and Assam Accords reached.

**Reactivation of the Proxy War**
In 1986, the Chinese were found to have surreptitiously intruded into and occupied Wangdung/Sumdrong Chu and Bisa Cane Bridge areas in Arunachal. The consequent Indian counter moves to try and evict them, as also the effects of extensive forward deployment of troops during '86–'87 along the Chinese borders to prevent any further Chinese incursions, resulted in increased tensions. There was also extensive Indian troop deployment along the western borders with a view to pose a threat to Pakistan to block infiltration which added to the already prevalent tension in the situation. By 1988, the Pakistani bomb reportedly was in place – 'Jehad' was ready for launch in Kashmir and the USSR umbrella had largely been neutralised with its collapse.

Unfortunately our pro-democracy and anti-military rule policy towards Myanmar, a military ruled state, led to misunderstandings with the country, with a result that Myanmar gave sanctuary to a number of north-eastern insurgent groups.

By early '90s Kashmir was in flames; NSCN had split and been reactivated; ULFA, NDFB, Tripura insurgents revitalised and nascent insurgency in Meghalaya born. We also saw a series of bomb blasts all over the country engineered by Pakistan as part of their proxy war.

## Rapprochement with the West and China

Fortunately, with USSR being marginalised, strained Sino-US relations, our progressive befriending of the West and the counter-productive effects of Jehad, western support to Pakistan waned. Also, as a result of foreign policy initiatives, the 'Border Peace and Tranquillity Accord' was signed with China. By the late '90s, the situation was brought under control and the 'Naga Ceasefire' came into effect after successful counter-insurgency operations.

By late 1997, Pakistan had realised that its strategy for wresting Kashmir and balkanisation of India by fomenting insurgency and violence all over the country had not worked. Further as they were no longer a frontline state to be used to defeat USSR, the West was losing interest in them. Terrorism all over India lacked popular support; counter-terrorism and insurgency operations were meeting with increasing success; people were getting more and more antagonistic to both Pakistan and Bangladesh having seen through their perfidy and everyone all over desperately wanted peace. In the north-east, a ceasefire with the NSCN (both groups) was achieved, the ULFA and NDFB were forced to shift their camps outside the country, and insurgency was brought well under control. In central India, the left extremists were contained and minority ethnic groups largely placated. In Jammu and Kashmir, tourism flourished again; there was development and economic progress; the vast majority of people had turned against Pakistan; Kashmir had almost vanished from international attention and the West was progressively becoming more supportive of India.

Pakistan desperately needed to bring itself back into the international focus, avenge 1971 through imposition of a major defeat on India, regain control over the local population of Kashmir through enhanced terrorism. And so the seeds of the Kargil War were sowed.

## The Kargil Conflict

Pakistan had become emboldened through testing of its nuclear weapons in 1998. Evoked and incited by the reasons discussed in the earlier paragraph, it therefore hatched a plan – to surreptitiously secure unoccupied heights across the Line Of Control (LOC) in the parts of Jammu and Kashmir that lay in the Kargil and southern glacier sectors of Ladakh. This, according to Pakistan, would prevent movement along India's strategic lifeline from Kashmir to Ladakh. This area was selected for this strategic route was closed from October to May every year due to heavy snowfall, thus this entire six months' period was available to achieve the objectives undercover. Since the area was also lightly held, with vast stretches only patrolled due to the inhospitable climatic conditions, securing these dominating heights would not pose major problems and also totally cut off Ladakh. It was anticipated that there would be strong reaction from Indian forces which would have to be brought in from Kashmir. This would then facilitate infiltrating J&K with large numbers of terrorists.

Indian Army reinforcements from the rest of India would also be drawn in to try and remove the intrusions and bring the situation under control, thereby reducing the possibility of a counter-strike elsewhere by the Indian forces. The nuclear shield, which was by then in place, was to be used psychologically to deter India from counter strikes into Pakistan. Notwithstanding this, the entire Pakistan Army was to mobilise and adopt a defensive posture to deal with Indian counter strikes. The entire operation was to be depicted as a Mujaheedin operation to liberate Jammu & Kashmir from Indian yoke. Instructions were also issued to the north-east insurgents, left extremists and sleeper cells amongst the minorities to reactivate and keep Indian security forces engaged to the optimum during this period so that minimum troops could be made available to reinforce Kargil. The intensity of activity in Jammu & Kashmir would automatically draw major international and media attention and hopefully their active intervention to resolve the Kashmir issue in Pakistan's favour.

Ironically, just before the plan was executed, the Indian Prime Minister had made a historic peace overture to Pakistan by travelling to Lahore to try and bring about peaceful settlement of the Indo-Pakistan dispute. While the Pakistani PM gave a commitment towards peaceful resolution, Pakistani armed forces, which had boycotted this meeting between the PM's, had already started putting the operation into effect. The plan was extremely audacious, well-conceived and brilliantly executed at the initial stages. Pakistan had however not correctly assessed the speed or violence of the Indian reactions, which were immediate and large-scale as well resulting in their eviction and defeat well before the onset of winter. The Kargil War evoked adverse international reaction to Pakistan. The Pakistanis were however successful in infiltrating large numbers of terrorists into both Kashmir and Jammu region and reactivating terrorism, which took another year and a half of very high intensity counter-terrorist operations to bring back under control.

## 9/11 and its Consequences

The events of 9/11 in the United States, US decision to strike at the terrorist infrastructure and invade Afghanistan, along with their coercing Pakistan into lending support as a frontline state in the US war against terrorism (Al Qaida and Bin Laden) and using Pakistan as a base for its operations into Afghanistan, put a different complexion to Pakistan's proxy war against India. Pakistan realised that the US needed their help desperately to track down Bin Laden who was then holed up in Afghanistan (with Pakistan's connivance) and would therefore be prepared to look the other way as long as it cooperated with the US, while it continued the proxy war with India.

## Attack on Indian Parliament

The previously discussed events therefore led to a pre-arranged terrorist strike on the Indian Parliament in December 2001 and simultaneously upgraded terrorist attacks in Kashmir. This amounted to crossing the threshold of Indian tolerance and resulted in mobilisation of the Indian Armed Forces and their deployment opposite Pakistan for war. As US troops were deployed in Pakistan, this brought immediate pressure on Pakistan and the US managed to prevent further escalation of violence and get Pakistan to take measures to stem terrorist activity propagated by it. It also resulted in the US having to grant a number of favours to Pakistan in terms of aid and announce it as a most favoured ally in spite of knowing only too well that Pakistan was the focal point of terrorism.

Meanwhile, on Pakistan's request Bangladesh had stepped up support to the north-east insurgents, consequently the situation in Assam, Tripura, Meghalaya and Manipur deteriorated. Pakistan and Bangladesh prevailed on the NSCN (I & M) to increase activity levels of their surrogate insurgent groups and to increase the tempo of their activity for Nagalim. The Left extremist and minority groups were also pressurised to increase their level of activities —there was an escalation in violence levels all over the country. The US war on terrorism also resulted in many of the terrorists including Al Qaida fleeing both Afghanistan and Pakistan to take sanctuary in Bangladesh. This aggravated the risk of increased Islamic fundamentalist activity to the north-east.

## Maoist Threat to Nepal

In Nepal, Maoist violence levels escalated as Pakistan, possibly with Chinese support, was out to try and destabilise Nepal, an old friend of India, and in doing so incite the Maoists who were anti-India. This also meant destabilising Indian Nepalese troops and Nepalese areas such as North Bengal and the Siliguri corridor; further Nepal was an important route for infiltrating vital Jehadi elements into India.

## Operations in Bhutan

The Government of Bhutan co-operated with India in December 2003 by launching operations to liquidate/destroy all NDFB/ULFA/KLO and other camps in Bhutan, with the Indian Army carrying out the border-sealing operations. The operation was a resounding success with all credit to the Bhutanese. The KLO and NDFB became totally marginalised and ULFA was forced to run back to its camps in Bangladesh and elsewhere. This facilitated giving the peace process with the Bodos a fillip in 2004 and brought temporary peace to Assam. Manipur and Tripura however continued to burn.

## Effects of US operations in Iraq

The US operations into Iraq created major problems for Pakistan as it was literally coerced by the US into continuing as its frontline state in its war against terrorism. It turned the Jehadis against President Musharaf. The Kashmiris also began to see Pakistan very clearly in a new light of being totally opportunist and not really being concerned about their interests – it also turned them somewhat towards India. Pakistan has consequently seen the winds of change and has now been forced to change its strategy towards India.

## Pakistan's New Game Plan

It is quite obvious that Pakistan's previous strategy has been seen through by the West and to stop Pakistan's earlier antics, it has put the country under tremendous pressure, while fully realising that West needs Pakistan's support. Pakistani overtures for talks and CBMs have obviously been made under western pressure. The talk of 'soft borders dialogues' and 'autonomy for Kashmir' is clearly part of a strategy to deceive, aimed to facilitate easier infiltration of terrorists and anti-social elements with the ultimate view to coercing the people of Kashmir into opting for Pakistan after a period of time. As they now feel that they have lost support of the people, the current phase of the terrorist attacks also appears to be targeted at the Kashmiri, to terrorise them into submission. We can and therefore must anticipate renewed efforts to upgrade violence levels in the future. This would, in all probability, be only the first step – the next would be to do the same in other Muslim populated areas in India including the north-east. The concept of soft borders would also facilitate demographic change much in the fashion of what has been done by Bangladesh – the overall strategy is to free all Muslims from Indian yoke and **balkanise India, not merely Kashmir**. This strategy would also obviously be fully supported by Bangladesh.

It therefore appears that the current plan is to pretend that they are serious about a peaceful resolution to the conflict. They have not stopped the proxy war – this continues unabated. This war has been extended to Nepal, through Left extremists, in India; in Punjab through a reactivated Babbar Khalsa; and by the insurgents with the support of ally Bangladesh in north-east. All this is apparently with the consent of the Chinese, who continue to aid and stand by Pakistan.

**Tilt towards the West**
Our recent alignment with the West undoubtedly irks China as they fear a strategic grouping of the US with its allies. This may well ultimately contribute to better relations with China as they may try to befriend India to counter the US.

**Need for a Balanced Foreign Policy**
Bangladesh becoming a haven for fundamentalism and sanctuary for extremists/insurgents can only bode ill; all this would mean continued proxy war. Maoist activities in friendly Nepal pose a direct threat to us and Bhutan – it is obvious as to who is supporting them. It therefore becomes imperative for us to have a balanced foreign policy, which ensures that we retain and increase our circle of friends, while making NO new enemies, and meet our challenges taking all possible consequences into account.

In this chapter, I have tried to highlight the effect our foreign policy has had with reference to the situation and developments in the north-east since Independence. I would like to conclude by stating that, while there may not be concrete proof in support of this analysis, circumstances, events and media reports over the period make a very valid circumstantial case. In the ensuing chapters, I will try and put across some views on problem resolution for the region.

# Section II
# RESOLUTIONS

# 9
# INDIA'S FOREIGN POLICY WITH REFERENCE TO THE NORTH-EAST

In the last section, we had an overview of the entire north-east region and its states. We also had a glimpse of the effects of the large numbers of servicemen/ex-servicemen residing in the region and the profound impact our foreign policy has had in contributing to the present situation in the north-east. We would now look at possible options for problem resolution, starting with our foreign policy.

**Duties of the State – National Security**
Whether in ancient treatises on statecraft, such as the *Arthashatra*, or the modern concept of 'nation state', or our Constitution, everywhere it is stated that it is the bounden duty of the nation to ensure **freedom and independence** to its citizens and protect their **core values** and **interests** – this is what is implied **by 'national security'**. An important ingredient of national security is the adoption of suitable policies and relations with other nations, which will contribute to security. It is however clear that we have not succeeded in this objective and are instead fighting a proxy war sponsored by the powers and hence the need to review our policy.

We need to face the fact that we currently have to survive in a unipolar world, with one superpower and a number of regional big powers, whose values and national interests may not coincide with ours. Whenever our policy has been on a collision course with them, we have reaped the consequences.

While we now appear to be following the correct course of seeking rapprochement in our relations, we need to critically examine as to how we can make these countries feel that our security is vital to their interests as well. I cite these instances – Saudi Arabia is now indispensable to the West for oil supplies; Pakistan has made the West feel it is indispensable to them in their 'war on terrorism'; Japan is indispensable to the West as a bulwark in East Asia; Pakistan has become indispensable to China to counter perceived Indian expansionism, and so on. We need to examine what we can offer these countries in exchange for peace and tranquillity, without endangering our independence or policy of self-reliance.

## The West
As far as the West is concerned, I would suggest that all we have to offer is trade and our huge markets – if the West can not find adequate markets for their goods and trade, economic collapse and hence loss of power is inevitable. Once western business interests are totally committed to us, we would then become vital for their survival. Though initiated, this is not yet the case; the West still looks the other way when our security is threatened.

## China
As far as China is concerned, the issues are much more complex in that, we both find it extremely difficult to trust each other after years of distrust/proxy war – I, for one, am extremely suspicious of the Chinese. How do we therefore find a way out of the impasse? Having been an avid China watcher over the last 44 years, I am of the view that today China has two major fears with reference to India – that we will team up with the West against it and secondly of economic failure due to its economy overheating as a result of excessive supply of money from investments, and loss of markets for its finished goods (consequently, its poor are getting poorer). It is therefore vital that China finds adequate entry into the Indian market coupled with increased trade. It is these two fields that will have to be exploited to the optimum – rather than simply being happy with talks with no worthwhile results and being subjected to proxy war. It is gratifying to note that we now appear to be on the threshold of better relations with China.

## Russia
We must also never forget or lose an old friend – Russia – which is still with us – and could definitely make a comeback in the not too distant future.

## Pakistan
As far as Pakistan is concerned, we need to face reality and accept that the Pakistani Army will never give up power in Pakistan easily – after

all 'Power Corrupts' – even if a civilian face is given to the government, it is the Army that will call the shots. We therefore have no option but to accept that the quarrel between us is primarily one of identity – including an Indian identity (are we Indian, secular or Hindu) – Kashmir, Assam, Punjab, Sindh only form small parts of the above. Does anyone truly believe that if we handed over Kashmir to Pakistan, the problem would be resolved? In my view, the problem resolution will take time and that also ultimately only**, by undoing Partition** – not through war – but **through discussions, economic activity, trade, cultural activity and people to people contact** and in the overall context through progressing towards an economic union of states. To make this possible it would be imperative to progress the above foreign policy options for the West and China suggested above, as that would ultimately apply pressure on Pakistan to resolve differences.

## Bangladesh

Bangladesh is progressively becoming fundamentalist and in many facets a failed state. Consequently, its people can not help but look for greener pastures across the border. This would continue to be supported by the Bangladeshi leadership in an attempt to further their philosophy of 'Lebensraum', with an ultimate aim of getting adjoining states to secede to Bangladesh. It is unlikely that border fences would ever stop the tide of migration, as it is next to impossible to police the entire land, river and sea borders effectively. The Bangladeshi leadership still holds the initial ideals that resulted in Partition – hemming them in with fences will only progressively increase animosity. Here again in my view, the only workable option to resolve differences with Bangladesh and to prevent them from turning fundamentalist is to undo the hatred created by the Partition through discussions to resolve problems, economic activity, trade, people to people contact and cultural interaction. With open borders, there will indeed be more migration – but surely that can be largely resolved by adopting a work-permit system. The practice of looking the other way in the interest of increasing our vote banks must stop. It also needs to be noted that Bangladesh is *de-facto* ruled by the Army and fundamentalists.

Bangladesh also has to be prevailed upon to stop its support and provision of sanctuary to various insurgent groups and integrate economically with the region. This can only be to its advantage as it would then have a ready market for both her labour and produce. It must also provide the region with transit facilities to the coast and West Bengal – particularly to south Assam and the other southern states of the region.

Our foreign policy options will need to cater to applying suitable pressures which may well include the threat of economic blockades, control over river waters and as a last resort, use of force, to keep our neighbours under control. Pressures also need to be applied on them through the western world as part of the war on terrorism.

### Nepal

The situation in Nepal today is disturbing – the king has thrown democracy to the winds; imprisoned or incarcerated the only viable political leadership available; more or less continued with a state of emergency to usurp all powers. Additionally, the Maoist extremists control a large part of the country. It is under these circumstances that we need to ensure that our friendship with Nepal is not ruined by policies that would sour relations with them in the long term. If we do not help them, we would only push them into China and Pakistan's lap – which is what they would be only too happy to see happen. We also cannot afford to sit back and allow the Maoist extremists to take control over Nepal in the manner they are now doing, as this would pose us a grave national security risk. We need to simultaneously help Nepal in restoring democracy and in taking other measures that would resolve their problems.

### Bhutan

Our friendship with Bhutan has matured and needs to be carried forward further – we should note that Bhutan had put itself to a great deal of trouble and risk; and been of tremendous help to us, in denying sanctuary to insurgents. We need to put in more effort towards assisting them in resolving problems they have so that a positive message goes across to our other neighbours.

### Sri Lanka

While our relations with Sri Lanka have been mixed, we need to put the past behind us and make a concerted effort to help them in resolving issues with the Liberation Tigers for Tamil Eelam (LTTE) and getting back to being a prosperous state, with no attitudinal problems with the 'Big Brother'. We also need to apply pressure on our southern states to desist from aiding the LTTE, if any, as it is this, more than anything else, would lead to souring our relations.

## Myanmar

While our terms with Myanmar have had major 'ups and downs', we must ensure good relations with them irrespective of the military rule. This must be done through greater interaction, trade, economic and cultural activity, and people to people contact. It is through such measures that we can help lessen antagonism between ourselves and the neighbours so that they can assist us in control of the drug menace to the north-east and in resolution of the socio-political problems related to ethnic sub-nationalism – particularly for ethnic groups that live on both the Indian and Myanmar sides of the border.

Myanmar must also be prevailed upon to dislodge ULFA and NSCN (K), NSCN (I&M) camps from their territories bordering Tirap and Changlang districts of Arunachal Pradesh; Manipuri insurgent groups who have taken sanctuary in the areas bordering Myanmar; Tripura groups that are located in the areas bordering Myanmar where they currently enjoy sanctuary.

## South-East Asia and the Middle East

We also need to befriend the South-East Asian countries, not only to improve economic ties and trade, but also to make them deny sanctuary to insurgent/terrorist groups, and stop them from using these groups as conduits for supply of surplus black market weapons and ammunition. Relations with the Middle-East countries need to be handled with a great deal of tact and diplomacy, to ensure denial of support to terrorists, international lobbying against us and guaranteed supplies of fuel.

In this chapter, I have tried to focus on aspects of foreign relations that need a review, with a view to bring peace and tranquillity to the north-east. In the next chapter, I will take an overview of the internal security issues that need reviewed to achieve similar peace dividends

# 10
# INTERNAL SOCIO-POLITICAL ASPECTS

## KEY ISSUES AND STEPS TOWARDS RESOLUTION

### Necessity for Review of Political Structure

The north-east has more than 500 different ethnic groups, many of whom feel neglected in some way or the other. Since it is a nation's chief responsibility to ensure the security and well-being of its people, it is the government's duty to ensure a socio-political structure that meets the aspirations of all. Provisions for this have already been made in the Sixth Schedule of the Constitution wherein it is stipulated that adequate measures may be instituted where necessary, to apply a suitable political structure based on existing tribal and local structures in the north-east with a view to protect the values and culture of the people of the region. We have however unfortunately faltered by foisting an alien and unworkable political model on the north-east.

### Balkanisation – A Mistake

Firstly, we must understand it is next to impossible to keep balkanising the existing states of the nation to meet demands of the numerous ethnic groups. The redrawing of state boundaries on so called ethnic lines, in the manner as has been done repeatedly, has been a major error as it has given further impetus to splintering the already fragile pluralistic civil society structure. It contributed to the creation of extremist groups like the ULFA, NDFB, NSCN, a number of Manipuri and Arunachal insurgent organisations and an upsurge in insurgency in the north-east. Also, in the states created from the '60s onwards, it resulted in ethnic fissures and strife, with examples being the rift between Khasis and Garos; Hmars, Paites, Chakmas, Brus and Mizos;

rift between the Dimasa, Karbis and Assamese and so on. The answer therefore lies in the realm of consociation politics as discussed below and not in balkanisation.

**Necessity for Consociation Politics**
It is therefore imperative to switch from the existing political structure of 'majority rule' with rigid territorial boundaries and neutralisation of traditional administrative institutions, wherein the majority ethnic group exercises a high degree of hegemony over its minorities, to one of 'consociation politics'. This calls for a very high degree of inter-ethnic cooperation in managing affairs in a highly pluralistic society whilst co-opting traditional institutions. It implies a coalition of the political elites of all the different ethnic groups within the existing political boundaries. It would give all the right of veto on issues of policy, proportional representation in most fields of administration and for allotment of funds, and a high degree of autonomy including traditional grass root and economic self-sufficiency for each ethnic group. If this is not done, minorities would continue to get a raw deal from the majority, with consequent agitation and insurgency.

**Removal of the Inner Line Policy**
The 'Inner Line' or 'Excluded Area' system evolved by the British today stands in the way of both integration and development, is discriminatory and hence needs to go. This is all the more so as it goes against the very tenets of consociation political structures, and contributes to splintering the civil society, particularly when ethnic groups have been divided by artificial political boundaries.

**Immigration/Migration**
Immigration/migration and its effect on changing demographic profiles is another aspect that needs to be attended to immediately as it is a major cause for agitation. The currently prevalent vote-bank politics of encouraging immigration for political gain must be forced to stop. Instead, a system of work permits needs to be introduced – in many cases with retrospective effect – while bearing in mind that the north-east is labour-deficient and would hence have to import labour for economic survival. Suitable legislation in this regard would have to be introduced and enforced.

## Limit Use of Force for Resolution of Political Problems

We invariably advise that development is essential for resolution of insurgency, while fully realising that development requires peace. It is indeed unfortunate that though we are a democracy with a partly federal form of government, some state governments have become defunct, shed their responsibility to Delhi and switched to use of force or counter-insurgency operations. They are attempting to achieve a military solution to the problem, without bothering to remember that the root causes of the insurgency need to be addressed through good governance and dialogue, coupled with stern action only when and where required. Consequently large numbers of security forces are deployed (which we can ill afford), to try and restore normalcy, innocent citizens are harassed and the government is accused of state-sponsored terrorism, which is then blamed on the security forces. Corruption is rampant with the militants often running a parallel government and economy through illegal taxes, smuggling and drug rackets – often in connivance with local politicians.

Control over all matters of even trivial policy is currently exercised through Delhi. This implies handling by bureaucrats and politicians sitting in Delhi, who are far removed from reality and do not even know the north-east or comprehend local situations – their portfolios are also changed very frequently – one can even quote situations where there were no officials to handle important subjects for long periods during crisis-ridden times. The requirement is to perhaps therefore delegate full authority to competent governors who can issue prompt directions within the overall policy framework issued by Delhi.

## Streamline Ministry of Home Affairs

Delhi needs to streamline their department for handling the north-east in the Ministry of Home Affairs and fill it with dedicated people closely integrated with the Ministry for North-Eastern Affairs.

## Necessity for Good Governance and Dialogue

In such an environment how can there be development? One frequently hears the refrain that the state response to defeat militancy through use of force does not work and is counter-productive. This is totally true – counter insurgency operations can only assist in temporarily bringing the situation under control to allow the state to function. It must be reiterated that, to resolve such militancy, there is no option but to ensure good governance coupled with dialogue – the military option must be used only when absolutely imperative for only an inescapable period and that also with people-friendly operations, and the complete weight of the government machinery behind it. Corruption and fund-raising by militants must be ruthlessly stamped out. The state police must be made effective, as it is they who must ultimately ensure law and order and not the armed forces of the centre. Unless all this is done simultaneously problem resolution is unlikely to succeed.

## The Mizoram Model

An example of a successful approach is the manner in which the Mizo insurgency was brought to an end – dilution of foreign support through creation of Bangladesh, concerted state and civil society (including the church) efforts towards improved governance and interaction with militants, successful people-friendly counter-insurgency operations (this was not initially the case) and the Mizo Accord.

## Stop Giving in to the Ethnic Groups that Agitate the Most

Delhi must also learn to see the north-east as a composite entity; pandering to the whims of one segment is likely to alienate the others – the answers do not lie in the politics of divide and rule, but in the consociation approach to politics. For instance, in the case of handling the NSCN (I&M) and Bodos, satisfying their demands will lead to alienation of other segments who live within the same boundaries.

## Use of ESM for Development

Considering the demographics of the SM/ESM of the north-east particularly in the states of Assam, North Bengal, Nagaland, Manipur and Mizoram, it is imperative that they be actively supported in their rehabilitation into civil life by the state and that the facet of their being trained, disciplined and nationally integrated manpower be exploited by the state to the optimum – sadly this is totally neglected. Impetus must be given also to organise them to produce the dividends of development on the lines of the erstwhile Army Development Groups created in the early '60s to help in the development of the then North East Frontier Tracts and to set up large business enterprises that would facilitate development and employment generation for themselves and their families.

**Ensuring more Effective and Good Administration**
We need to ensure that good, dedicated officers of the IAS, IPS and other central/state services including the armed forces are entrusted with grass-root administration and development in the north-east. Today, many of these officers fail to rise up to their duties in society and try to evade service in remote areas by obtaining deputations repeatedly to stay away from them, while trying to obtain all the privileges and perks that go with difficult assignments. There is also a need to educate our politicians, bureaucrats, intellectuals, teachers/professors and the public at large on the north-east and its people – there is not a single textbook on any subject, which talks about the north-east. Today in places like Delhi, a north-easterner is often asked whether he is from China or Thailand. North-eastern women are considered fair game for eve teasing because they dress differently and look different. This cannot be integration – there has be to far deeper amalgamation of cultures if we really want to see ourselves as the proud democracy we claim to be.

In view of the fact that the subject is sensitive, I must reiterate that the views expressed are my own and that they should be considered in totality and not in isolation of each other, in the form of suggestions for serious consideration. I must also express the view that we are a young and relatively inexperienced nation – mistakes are therefore inevitable, but must be remedied with a view to fulfil our dream of being a great nation.

In this chapter, I have tried to highlight the major socio-political aspects of the north-east that need to be addressed towards problem resolution. In the next chapters, I would be addressing economic, developmental and politico-military aspects of problem resolution for the north-east.

# 11
# ECONOMIC ASPECTS

### The Present Politico-Economic Model
The present policy framework for the region is based on a centrally controlled political economy and a cultural approach, adjusted with a regional planning model. It is implemented mainly through the Planning Commission and the North East Council. In this model, the north-east states are required to submit project proposals to the North East Council headquartered in Shillong after taking aspects related to their culture and traditions into consideration. These are then considered at the Council headquarters and then placed before the Council, which consists of the governors, chief ministers, other relevant ministers and bureaucrats of all north-east states, who jointly take a decision on projects, which are to be submitted to the Planning Commission at Delhi. These are considered by the commission and submitted to the government for approval. Projects that will ultimately be executed are dependent on release of funds by Delhi. In reality, nothing goes as per the projections as the system gets short-circuited by states approaching Delhi directly and vested interests coming into play.

### Benefits of the Model
All north-eastern states have been declared "Special Category States", which entitle them to 90% of central assistance as grants and 10% as loan. Some public sector units have also been set up. Industrial licensing, concessional finance, investment subsidy, growth centres, and freight equalisation for some industries have been used to try and promote industrial development.

### Problems
Despite huge investments, economic development has not happened – it has instead contributed to a politically-led distribution-oriented process, with a result that natural resources, profits and savings are moving out to higher productivity regions. In simple terms, as the system is frequently

short circuited due to political considerations, the infrastructure required by the north-east to be economically viable has simply not been executed. Thus natural resources flow out of the region to be processed elsewhere and return as manufactured items at high prices due to tenuous communications links and rampant corruption. The total dependence on central funds and direction has also promoted passiveness amongst the people. As there is very little infrastructure that would provide employment, there is now a government monopoly on it which is destroying the work ethics of both the economy and region.

Economic failures which can be largely enumerated are:

- Most financial receipts are from Delhi;
- State revenues are almost non existent;
- Unplanned expenditure including that spent on security is very high;
- In spite of being totally agricultural, the region is deficient of food due to destructive land utilisation patterns in the form of 'slash and burn' or *'jhoom'* type of cultivation and faulty land policy wherein all land in tribal belts belong to the community and not to individuals. Consequently the incentive to profit does not exist;
- Most industrial units are sick; private enterprise is limited; the region is labour scarce and consequently needs to import labour;
- The region is power-deficient in spite of having enormous potential;
- Infrastructure, particularly in the hill regions, is woefully inadequate.

## Black Economy

There is a parallel and huge 'black' economy (in the form of extortion, smuggling and illegal taxes) run by terrorist organisations in collusion with the authorised administrative structure. In almost all the states, except Sikkim, North Bengal and to a certain extent, Mizoram, there is a very high degree of corruption and siphoning off government money, all of which seriously impede economic progress and development.

## Resolution of Economic Crisis

### *Need for Review*
While there are many who would say that it is insurgency that is impeding progress, the corollary to this is also true – development would

greatly assist in removing some of the root causes for insurgency. It is therefore clear that the economic policy and its execution need review.

## *Requirement for Curbs*

While there can be no two opinions on the requirement for the northeast to switch from the present centrally-controlled economic system, to that of a regional market-driven economy, with large-scale private investments in co-operation with the state governments, this cannot succeed if the parallel 'black economy' is not curbed. Whether it is Assam, Nagaland, Manipur, Tripura or Arunachal, the insurgents collect taxes, carry out extortion, take a share of all government contracts, extract protection money, and run arms/drug/timber/smuggling rackets at gunpoint, in many cases in connivance with politicians, bureaucrats/government officials.

This has strangled market-driven forces and the private sector – it in fact instigates the otherwise law-abiding youth to take the easy way out to make money through extortion. In Nagaland, the NSCN (I&M) openly extorts so-called taxes from all sources, including politicians, government servants and public sector undertakings, with full knowledge of the authorities that simply look the other way. They are indulging in gun running, drug smuggling, illegal utilisation of forest produce; control illegal trade on the Myanmar border; run business enterprises abroad. The doles made by Delhi to Nagaland are finding their way into NSCN coffers.

The excuse given for not clamping down on such activities is that such an action would disrupt the peace process. Consequently the incentive for private enterprise or investment in Nagaland is non-existent. Extorted funds are used to strengthen the NSCN, arm more insurgents and make the organisation strong enough to further their demands if so required, and line the pockets of their leadership and politicians/bureaucrats who have a nexus with them. Under these circumstances how can Nagaland develop or become economically self-sufficient?

Those in authority need to urgently review their handling of this situation. We find similar situations in all the other insurgency-affected states – though not to this degree or as blatantly, except in Manipur where the situation is much worse, as the common man has to satisfy the demands of many more insurgent groups. The primary focus and strategy of the national counter-insurgency efforts of all agencies therefore need to switch primarily to denial of funds to the insurgent. Without funds, insurgency will die out on its own accord.

**Curbing the Insurgent-Politician-Businessman Nexus**
The nexus between the politician/bureaucrat/government official and the insurgents and the linked corruption need to be tackled ruthlessly and on a war footing – even if this implies Presidents Rule being imposed and the replacement of at least part of the administrative machinery in certain states. There is also a need to clamp down on industry and businessmen in the region as they have contributed to the insurgent exchequer through extortion and payment of protection money and failed to report the same. There are also numerous cases where the businessmen are banking and investing insurgent group funds and carrying out *hawala* transactions for the insurgent groups for a profit. These businessmen literally control the finances of the north-eastern states and are in league with both the state administration and the insurgents. This amounts to treason and needs to be very sternly dealt with.

***Trimming the State Apparatus and Taxation***
There is a requirement to drastically trim the state apparatus to achieve economy in non-developmental expenditure, with state governments switching to the role of being facilitators. State revenues have to be increased if necessary through imposition of taxes so as to make funds available for development and to make their economies self-sustaining. Presently the hill states have no income tax levies. The entire region has been living on 'doles', which is damaging the psyche of the north-easterner – this needs to be progressively stopped and instead encouragement given to entrepreneurship and employment created in the private sector. It also needs to be noted that these doles have contributed to easy funding of insurgent movements.

***Concentration on the Agricultural Sector***
The livelihood of the majority of the population in the north-east is agriculture – focus of economic development must shift to reform in the agricultural sector and be driven by market forces. This must include horticulture, floriculture, and commercial produce of bamboo/other cash crops which will make the region self-sufficient in generating its

own food. Industrial development should target this sector and reform the existing industry to make it more productive. Slash and burn cultivation, wherein all vegetation on the agricultural plot is first burnt, then allowed to lie fallow for sometime and followed by sowing of seeds, must be prohibited and land laws amended from the existing community ownership to private ownership. Similarly the 'Inner Line' must go – how can there be investment if investors cannot enter the area and land cannot even be made available on lease? Investment on power generation, water supply and road/rail/air network and other essential infrastructure is urgent and inescapable.

### *Industrialisation*
With the north-east being relatively abundant in natural resources, effort must be made to industrialise it, to change it from being a primary product-exporting region to a finished product-exporting region. The industrial climate needs to be made more efficient and effective through investment, privatisation and encouraging entrepreneurship.

### *Labour Policy*
As the region is labour deficient, there is no option but to import labour from outside – this is one of the main reasons for immigration. A rational policy will have to be framed to ensure availability of labour while ensuring simultaneously that the demographic balance is not upset.

### *Foreign Trade*
Illegal cross border trade needs to be legalised and revenue accrued. This could be done in conjunction with declaring specified areas along the borders free trade zones. Trade with the neighbouring countries needs to be enhanced/opened including China, Bangladesh, South-East Asia, Nepal, with a view to integrating the north-east with the global market. Trade transit agreements must be arrived at with Bangladesh to balance the costs of transportation along the tenuous lines of communication with the rest of India.

### *Higher and Technical Education*
While general literacy levels in the north-east are high, higher education levels are low. This needs urgent redressal as the north-east is woefully

short of skilled personnel in almost all fields. It is due to this that unemployment levels are high, which only fuels the feeling of neglect and deprivation further. Suitable measures that will help create employment are therefore imperative.

# 12
# POLITICO – MILITARY ASPECTS

**Causes of Insurgency**
Insurgency is an armed rebellion of a section of a population – invariably the minorities in a region – against the policies of the state and its established government. The causes of insurgency are invariably due to social, political or economic reasons. On the other hand, it is the primary duty of the state, particularly in a democracy, to ensure the well-being and security of its citizens. This implies that the state must make itself aware of its people's grievances and redress them well in time to avoid conflict situations. It is apparent that insurgency occurs in most cases, due to poor governance and neglect of minorities, including the constitutional provisions which allow them to air their grievances, and have the same redressed.

**Importance of Political Resolution**
All the insurgencies in the north-east require political resolution. In Tripura, the tribals need a suitable package, which will guarantee protection of their political, cultural, social rights and economic well-being. In Assam, the issue of migration, economic development and protection of rights of the minorities needs to be addressed. In Meghalaya, the issues of migration, economic development and removal of causes of ethnic rivalry also needs to be looked at. In Nagaland and Arunachal, the issues of the NSCN's demands, protection of the cultural, social and political rights of the tribes and economic development have to be addressed. In Manipur, the ethnic strife, rights of all ethnic groups, provision of good and impartial governance and economic development have to be dealt with. In North Bengal, the rights of the minorities and their economic development need to be handled. In all cases, a combination of good governance, redressal of grievances, limiting corruption, economic development, military operations, negotiations and denial of foreign support is imperative to end the insurgencies.

## Stoppage of Foreign Support

It must be reiterated that the issue of foreign support to the insurgents must be addressed at the highest level on priority, as without it being brought under control, insurgency will in all likelihood continue. A simple analysis of the situation post-1971 operations in East Pakistan would reveal that all insurgencies in the north-east went on to a very low key due to lack of foreign support, till the military take-over of Bangladesh in 1978.

Before we analyse the use of force or military operations by the state, let us first examine which instruments of the state are most suited to deal with crises of such nature.

## Use of Military Force to Quell Insurgency

I will not go into the detailed causes of each of the north-east insurgencies, as these have already been discussed in preceding chapters. In all these cases however the policy of the government has been to try to quell the rebellion using military force, without adequately addressing the causes for grievance, except in North Bengal where political action was in some cases been relatively prompt. In Mizoram which was ultimately a success story, it is only after many years of insurgency that the government policy switched to socio-economic-political resolution of the conflict, coupled with the denial of foreign support and military operations. In this context, it needs to be understood that long periods of use of pure military force are always counter-productive, as it only serves to alienate the population further, since there would always be some infringement of human rights and harassment of even those who are innocent during such operations. Further, if the authorities do not address the causes of grievance simultaneous to the military operations, the degree of alienation increases multi-fold.

## Principles of Counter-Insurgency

It must always be noted that it is the duty of the state to resolve the conflict and not the Security Forces that have been charged only with quelling the armed rebellion. The **cardinal principles** in such operations which apply to all agencies of the state are:

- **Try and win the hearts and minds of the people** affected by insurgency through resolution of grievances, good and responsive governance and people-friendly operations simultaneously

- **Denial of foreign support** to the insurgents through both foreign policy options and military operations where feasible
- **Neutralisation of the insurgents** through conduct of sustained operations, with a view to apprehend them and also to deny them help from the public who form sustenance and support bases for conduct of negotiations.

It must be remembered always that we are dealing with a misguided section of our own citizens and NOT the enemy. Unfortunately, in almost all cases our government has followed a policy of leaving the 'forces' it has deployed to quell any armed rebellion, to deal with the insurgency and washed its hands off the responsibility of directing and co-ordinating this conjoint effort. How can a socio-political-economic conflict be resolved purely through the use of military force? It is for this reason that most insurgencies have been long drawn affairs with no solution in sight.

**Police assisted by CPOs must handle Insurgency**
There has been a furore in the media over the necessity to repeal the Armed Forces Special Powers Act (AFSPA). It is imperative to familiarise readers with the reasons why the armed forces are employed for "Counter Insurgency (CI)" operations, how they operate, the special powers they are conferred and the necessity for all these. There is need also to analyse the role of the state police/armed police/para-military/central police organisations in such operations.

It must be remembered always that the Army is the ultimate instrument of the state and must be deployed to deal with armed rebellion by a section of the population only as a last resort, when everything else fails. It would always be desirable for the states to deal with such problems using the state police forces as they are the most suited in all respects for such tasks. This would obviously mean modernising and training them suitably as they are currently not equipped to deal with such situations – there can be no doubt that no one can know the area or the people or their problems better than the local policemen, who are from that area and of the people. In case there is a lack of resources, the police could be backed up by Central Police Organisations (CPOs)/Para Military Forces (PMF), who should preferably function under the control of the police. Our CPOs/PMF unfortunately lack the ethos, culture, training and organisation to function in such an environment, which needs to be rectified. It is only when the state police and the state administration have been totally subverted that the operational situation should be handed over to the CPOs/PMF.

### Role of the Armed Forces

The armed forces (the Army, Navy, Air Force and their auxiliaries) are an instrument of the state. Their primary role is to defend the nation's territorial integrity and vital interests. This implies defence against external armed aggression. The armed forces also have a secondary role, which is to aid civil power to maintain and restore law and order in cases of strife, violence and natural calamities and catastrophes. Assistance in natural calamities is beyond the purview of this article and is not addressed further.

It is important to note that the armed forces are called upon to maintain and restore law and order only when the situation is beyond control of the police, armed police and para-military forces/central police organisations. In the event of such an emergency, the armed forces operate in cooperation and conjunction with the civil administration. In situations, wherein employment is to bring rioting, communal riots and so on under control, the Armed Forces are employed under the provisions of Indian Criminal Procedure Code (CrPC) 130–131. This injunction stipulates their requisition by a magistrate, wherein police are present but have lost control. Only after the magistrate has handed them over the situation, can they take action adhering strictly to the principle of use of minimum force which dictates doing as little injury to person and property as may be considered necessary.

### *Army Deployment*

It must be reiterated that the Army should be deployed only when the CPOs/PMF are unable to handle the situation – and that also only for a specified period of time to bring the situation under control to allow the state machinery to function.

### *State Backing in Counter Insurgency Operations*

It must be appreciated that when the state is constrained to deploy the Army to bring armed rebellion under control, the Army must be given the full backing of the state in all its facets. This includes special powers, authority and legal protection to deal with the situation where the police and the administration have been rendered ineffective due to subversion, a unitary command and control structure with the Army at the helm of control, and with the state's resources where necessary placed at the Army's disposal. This implies simultaneous effort by the state to redress the causes of the conflict and re-establish its instruments of administration and control. It also implies that the state would dispense with the services of the Army as soon as the situation has been controlled adequately for the state machinery to function.

## *Army not to be asked to perform Police Functions*

The Army should not be expected to perform tasks which can be performed by CPOs/PMF/Police such as policing of ceasefires, security duties, law and order functions, crowd and mob control and so on. In my view, the Army does not need to handle the situation in Manipur till Delhi enunciates a clear and rational policy on how the situation is to be handled. At the moment all Meiteis, including the state government and the bureaucrats perceive the Army's operations to be targeted solely against the Meiteis while the actual villains – NSCN (I&M) and their surrogates are going scot-free, with the consequence that the Army and the Assam Rifles are being much maligned due to no fault of theirs. Similarly in Assam and Tripura, consequent to successful counter-insurgency operations, the situation is well within the capability of the state police to handle backed by adequate CPOs/PMF. The Assam Rifles can also handle Nagaland, as long as the ceasefire holds and no action is taken to clamp down on NSCN (I&M)'s extortion and other illegal activities (such a clamp-down may result in a breakdown of the ceasefire). Notwithstanding the above, in case the Army is withdrawn from counter-insurgency operations in any of the states, it is imperative that it maintains a strong permanent presence in each of them so as to always keep abreast of the situation, act as threats to insurgents, and be readily available should the situation deteriorate.

## *Method of Operation*

When the Army has to be deployed for such operations where the state machinery has been subverted, there is usually an intelligence failure. It therefore initially deploys company-sized groups (about 100 men) in seemingly important places all over the "Disturbed Area" and sets about trying to gain intelligence in conjunction with the government machinery to the extent feasible. There are also times the when state government has fled from the area and there is complete breakdown of all operations, especially intelligence. Intelligence is gathered by dominating the entire area through small groups of patrols and ambushes, arresting suspects and carrying out searches of suspected places. At this stage, due to an intelligence void it is more than natural that some innocent people may undoubtedly be harassed. However, as intelligence is rebuilt, operations become more specific and lesser number of innocent people get affected.

### *The Armed Forces Special Powers Act*
When there is a state of armed insurrection, and the civil machinery has broken down, due to coercion and subversion (wherein the authorities and the people are too terrorised to function normally) and the armed forces are called to restore normalcy, the provisions of the Cr PC are inadequate for the armed forces to operate. It is to cater to such situations that the Parliament has conferred the armed forces with certain special powers. These powers can only be exercised after:

- the governor of a state has declared the area 'Disturbed' through notification, under Sec 3 of the AFSPA,
- the state government has requested for intervention of the armed forces to restore normalcy,
- the central government has approved the above,
- and the armed forces deployed are in 'aid' of civil power which implies that the forces are operating at the request of the government.

### *Main Provisions of the AFSPA*
The main provisions of AFSPA are the following:

- Any Commissioned (Class 1 Gazetted Officer), Warrant (Class 2 Gazetted Officer) or Non-commissioned (Class 2 Non Gazetted Officer) Officer in the armed forces may in a 'Disturbed Area', for maintenance of public order, after giving due warning, fire upon (causing even death) to any person acting against any law/order.
- Prohibition of assembly of five or more persons or carrying of weapons, or ammunition or explosive substances.
- Destruction, if necessary, any arms dump, prepared/fortified position/shelter from which armed attacks may be made, or any structure used as a training camp/hideout for armed volunteers.

- Arrest without warrant of any person who has committed/is likely to commit a cognisable offence, and use of force as may be necessary to affect the arrest; enter and search without warrant any premises to make the arrest or to recover any person believed to be wrongfully confined, or any property suspected to be stolen, or any arms, ammunition or explosive substances unlawfully kept. Use of force for all the above purposes is sanctioned.
- Under the AFSPA, all persons arrested are to be handed over to the nearest police station with minimum delay, together with a report on the circumstances of arrest. The AFSPA provides protection to persons operating under the AFSPA for immunity from prosecution, without prior sanction of the central government

## *Areas currently declared Disturbed*

The areas which have been declared 'Disturbed' and where the Army/Assam Rifles/Border Security Force (BSF)/Central Reserve Police Force (CRPF)/state armed police have been deployed are most of Assam, part of Tripura, part of Arunachal Pradesh, Nagaland, Manipur and a 20-km belt bordering Assam cutting through Meghalaya, Arunachal Pradesh and Mizoram.

## *Clarifications on the Act by the Supreme Court*

The Supreme Court has issued certain clarifications on the provisions sanctioned by the centre to the armed forces. They are:

- Use of minimum force must dictate all actions; if fire is to be opened it must first be ascertained that it is essential for maintenance of public order and that due warning has been given.
- There should be no harassment of innocent people, or destruction of property of the public, or unnecessary entry into the dwellings of people not connected with unlawful activities.
- As far as possible the armed forces should co-opt civil police during execution of operations.
- They should not arrest/search women without the presence of a woman police officer to the best extent possible under the given circumstances.
- They should hand over arrested persons to the police with minimum possible delay – preferably within 24 hours, along with a detailed report of the arrest and all items seized in the operation.

Based on these directions of the Supreme Court, the armed forces' authorities have issued comprehensive 'Do's and Don'ts' to all personnel deployed on counter-insurgency operations and take stringent disciplinary action against all those who fail to comply with the provisions of these laws.

### Civilians' Grouse

Over a period of time there have been widespread agitation by civil society in a number of Disturbed Areas over the issue of excesses that have allegedly been committed under the AFSPA and there have been demands for its withdrawal.

Generally the issues civilians have been agitating against in the media are:

- sweeping powers have been given to the armed forces and that there are inadequate checks and balances against their misuse,
- even non-commissioned officers have these powers – they should be limited to commissioned officers only,
- civil police should be co-opted for operations; no arrest or searches should be carried out without warrant – immediate handing over of the apprehended to police should be ensured,
- far too many innocent people are being killed/harassed; women are being arrested without the presence of women police, raped and even killed in fake encounters,
- many of the alleged encounters are fake,
- human rights are being blatantly violated,
- those defence personnel who are guilty of disregarding the law must be brought to book.

### The Army Point of View

While taking the civilians' seriously, we must also remember that the Army has no desire to be operating against their brethren and have been directed by the government to perform an unpleasant duty. Insurgency occurs due to poor governance – and then spirals into a situation wherein the state machinery has lost control and been coerced and subverted into doing the insurgent's bidding. Restoring such situations should preferably be the task of central para-military/police organisations. Though these organisations have been so chartered and raised in very large numbers for this task, they are relatively ineffective due to poor leadership, ethos and training. Ultimately and unfortunately, it is the Army that gets deployed into an extraordinary situation, for which it has no legal powers of search, apprehension or connected police powers unless it is bestowed powers under the AFSPA.

Once deployed it is faced with situations and circumstances as follows:

- What does the Army do when the state machinery has fled, or at least part of the police and administration is subverted and liable to leak out plans? How does the Army ferret out insurgents in a void of intelligence from the police? It has to create its own intelligence and act on it. An attempt to obtain a warrant may mean a leak and escape of insurgents – attempts to get the police to accompany are frequently met with a reply of inadequate resources, or in some cases non-cooperation for fear of retaliation by insurgents. Under such circumstances how does the Army co-opt the police into its operations?
- The Army has only a limited number of commissioned officers – it therefore relies on efficient Non Commissioned Officers (NCOs) with years of experience. The Army has no option but to employ these NCOs to lead some teams/patrols – failing which operations would come to a grinding halt and the situation would deteriorate.
- The Army tries to avoid arresting women in the absence of woman police, however in case no women police are immediately available and the requirement is to immediately apprehend a hard-core female terrorist, where is the option?
- As regards allegations of rape and fake encounters – all such allegations are investigated and the personnel when found guilty are dealt with. It has been the Army's experience from these investigations that majority of these allegations have been false and are made by those with vested interest in curtailing the scope of the Army's operations. Notwithstanding all these issues, the effort is always to use minimum force.
- With regard to the Army being given sweeping powers – how does the Army bring such situations under control without these powers? Of course, there are checks and balances – every incident complained about or reported by the media is investigated and guilty persons, if any, are brought to book.
- It must always be remembered that the Indian Army is a 'Peoples' Army' tasked to operate against its misguided brethren. It is dealing with extraordinary situations in a total void – obviously

some human rights would be curtailed – but in most cases they would be more than respected.
- When insurgents feel they are cornered, they open fire first – in the Army's case it must first satisfy itself that public order is at stake, issue a warning and then only resort to retaliatory fire – consequently many soldiers die – where are the Army's human rights?

I have already explained the volatile situation prevailing in Manipur in a preceding chapter – those with vested interests (including externally visible elements of militant groups many of whom form Human Rights Organisations as a front) are now exploiting incidents that occur during operations.

### *Necessity for AFSPA*
The situation in Manipur is particularly acute with about 6000–8000 armed insurgents violating public order, committing murder and widespread extortion – the Army and other forces are deployed to try and restore normalcy. How do they do so without the legal powers conferred by AFSPA? Also, any dilution in AFSPA will impinge on the ability to deal with such situations and therefore have serious ramifications at the national level. It is interesting that after the AFSPA was withdrawn from Imphal, there has been a major increase in insurgent violence. Notwithstanding the necessity of AFSPA, undoubtedly with a large number of troops committed, there are bound to be mistakes and the odd black sheep – those guilty of violating orders – are brought to book, some perhaps quietly to avoid embarrassment.

### *Prevention of Terrorism Act (POTA)*
It has been found from experience by all the security forces of the country that the existing laws of the land, namely the CrPC and the Indian Penal Code (IPC), are inadequate in terms of legal provisions to be able to investigate, book and proceed against people indulging in acts of terrorism coupled with armed insurrection of a large scale. It is for this reason that we earlier had the MISA and TADA that were repealed under pressure from the politicians and human rights activists on grounds that its provisions were being grossly misused primarily to resolve issues of political vendettas. We thereafter had a fairly long period of void –consequently, there was tremendous pressure from the security forces to reinstate such an act as they were finding it

extremely difficult to investigate and prosecute cases of terrorism and organised crime. We therefore saw the institution of the Prevention of Terrorism Act come into being during the tenure of the National Democratic Alliance (NDA) government. Congress-ruled states refused to apply POTA and instead enacted a similar law called Prevention of Organised Crime (POCA), which was a watered down version of the POTA with safeguards built in to prevent its abuse particularly against politicians – the POCA however does not meet the needs of handling terrorism adequately.

We now hear that the POTA is likely to be repealed by the central government on the grounds of its misuse for political vendettas. Though human rights activists are applauding this action, how do the security forces handle cases of terrorism and armed insurrection adequately? Even under the AFSPA, the individual who is arrested has to be booked under some Act – inadequacy in provisions will only allow terrorists to go scot-free! Today we are talking about the international effort in the 'War on Terrorism' – almost every country in the world has enacted tough and special laws to deal with this menace. By repealing this Act for political reasons, the government would be blameworthy for disarming its security forces that have to carry out counter-terrorist operations. It could instead either enact a separate law to this end or alternatively amend the existing law by building in safeguards.

### *Human Rights and the Security Forces*
We are one of the few countries in the world to have a Constitution that specifically safeguards human rights. In addition, we have National and State Human Rights Commissions with legal and judicial powers to deal with complaints on violation of human rights. We also have hyperactive human rights organisations including those who act on the behest of the terrorists and an equally hyperactive media whose reportage borders in many cases on sensationalism. The Indian Army also has its own Human Rights Organisation (the only country in the world to do so) that investigates human rights complaints and in turn both directs prosecution where necessary and reports to the National Human Rights Commission. Further, all commanders are vested with the powers to initiate action against persons guilty of such violations of conduct. The Army also has an excellent record of upholding human rights. All complaints, media reports and cases of such misconduct are *suo moto* investigated and those guilty are promptly dealt with –

some possibly quietly without any publicity with a view to protect the Army's image. Under these circumstances, it must be pointed out that the system has adequate safeguards built in – why do essential laws then need to be repealed?

In this chapter, I have tried to highlight major aspects of the politico-military policy related to the handling of insurgency in the north-east, the Army's role, its employment in CI operations, the provisions of the AFSPA, issues put across by various agencies for its repeal, my views on the subject as a retired soldier and necessity for its retention. It clearly emerges that insurgency must be prevented through good governance and should it unfortunately occur, socio-political and economic measures must go hand in hand with military operations to achieve problem resolution.

# 13

# VIEWS ON PROBLEM RESOLUTION FOR THE NORTH-EAST

**General Overview**

In the preceding chapters, I familiarised readers with the north-east, the insurgency, issues of servicemen/ex-servicemen, and my views on arriving at viable solutions related to foreign, internal, economic and politico–military policies. I will now cover other aspects of problem resolution, within the overall canvas of the region.

I must begin by reiterating that steps towards problem resolution have to be considered for the region in its entirety and not in isolation, as methods of resolution for one state would in all probability impinge on the well-being of another. Simplistic answers (as is the view in Delhi) that resolution of problems with the NSCN (I&M) will automatically resolve insurgency in the entire region as the NSCN (I&M) is the mother organisation to most of the insurgent groups, is a total fallacy. Giving in to their demands would agonise the sensibilities of the ethnic groups of all the neighbouring states.

## ISSUES SPECIFIC TO ASSAM

**Development in Assam**

Assam is the hub of the region – unless there is major economic progress, the problems of the state cannot be resolved. This implies that the highest priority and financial assistance/investment for development in all its facets must be given to Assam, so that it can be developed into an industrial and agricultural base for finished products and infrastructure for the entire region. The NEC should control this to ensure that the entire region's requirements are met.

## Resolution of ULFA problem Dependent on Resolution of Other Issues

Assam's ULFA problem can only be resolved by a multi-pronged approach of:

- dialogue and problem resolution with militants,
- dealing with migration,
- economic development,
- denial of support from Bangladesh,
- curbing corruption and clamping down on 'black' economy
- resolution of land and other disputes with neighbouring states.

## Talks with ULFA

As a result of ongoing counter-insurgency operations and public pressure on ULFA for peace, reports indicate that talks with the ULFA are finally going to see the light of day. While this is a significant and gratifying development, what is disturbing are the media reports that the talks may be unconditional and that one of the ULFA's pre-requisites is that their arrested leaders be released prior to the commencement of talks.

## Key Issues

While talks with the insurgents are imperative to identify and resolve grievances, those concerned with policy decisions regarding these talks, must take note of the errors that were committed in relation to the ceasefire and talks in progress with the NSCN (I&M), ULFA's linkages to the ISI, Pakistan's proxy war strategy, Bangladeshi support to north-eastern insurgent groups, the prevalent situation in Assam and the fact that elections in Assam are round the corner.

## Talks with Present Leadership Amount to Talking to Pakistan

While keeping the above in mind, we must also remember that we cannot and must not apply the same yardstick for talks with the ULFA as are in progress with the NSCN (I&M) – the issues are totally different. While the ISI and Bangladeshi intelligence (DGFI) have undoubtedly assisted the NSCN (I&M) in the past and continue to do so, the NSCN (I&M) leadership and its cadres are not directly controlled by the ISI – indeed they have proved time and again they function with a mind of their own and operate in their own interests. On the other hand, the ULFA as also many other groups are totally under absolute control of the ISI and DGFI. It must be noted that ULFA's leadership has been given sanctuary in Bangladesh and has vast capital invested in businesses in that country and abroad with concurrence of the Bangladesh government, DGFI and the ISI. ULFA cannot touch this capital without the concurrence of all these agencies; their personal security in Bangladesh is provided by these agencies; the families of these leaders and indeed the leaders themselves are puppets controlled by these agencies; they are therefore in no position to take a single decision of importance on their own accord. Any talks by the Indian government with the ULFA therefore will be talks controlled by the ISI/DGFI and amount to talks on Pakistan and Bangladesh terms!

**Issues related to Errors in Handling NSCN**
In 1997 the NSCN (I&M) was brought to its knees –this is what brought them to the negotiating table and the current ceasefire. We then mishandled the terms of the ceasefire and its management. We have allowed the NSCN (I&M) to thereafter recruit a very large number of cadres, train, equip and arm them –they are now over 5000 armed and trained cadres strong; we have then allowed them to carry out extensive and rampant extortion and take control of the whole of Nagaland and the claimed areas in the neighbouring states. Today they dictate terms to all and literally govern these areas illegally and are largely culpable for the situation in Manipur. Nothing happens in these areas without their consent. They hold the security forces, responsible for policing the ceasefire, to ransom with a threat of breaking/abrogating the ceasefire. Today the NSCN (I&M) talks to the Government of India from a position of strength, blackmails the Government into acceding to their demands as has recently happened after some of their men were killed by the SF in neighbouring states and we are culpable of having permitted that to happen.

Currently the situation in Assam is similar to that in Nagaland in 1997 – ULFA is almost on its knees. It has been thrown out of Bhutan; it lacks popular support; the people of Assam are yearning for peace and development; the ULFA in Assam is in disarray, with only its Eastern Region (upper Assam) cadres operating out of camps in Myanmar alongside the NSCN (K) and Bangladesh, though under intense pressure from the security forces. Under such circumstances it would be foolhardy if policy makers release the interned ULFA leadership and go into a ceasefire mode on the pattern we did with NSCN (I&M).

**Issue of Elections**

Undoubtedly talks with ULFA and a temporary peace in Assam would be to the credit of the present Assam government and score heavily in their favour for the forthcoming elections. The political scenario in Assam however need to be noted –there will undoubtedly be a split in the AGP which can not but help the present government. The BJP in Assam is also unlikely to contribute much of opposition. Whilst Supreme Court's repeal of the IMDT Act has resulted in a number of the Muslims of Assam banding together politically and threatening the ruling party that they would vote against them if their interests were not protected, there is every possibility that they would ally with the ruling party in their own interest. There would be probably some ULFA sponsored candidates –but is it worth the present parties while in grouping with them or in trying to get ULFA's support, when they have the capability to win the elections on their own steam and taking a decision in favour of ULFA and the ISI in detriment to national interests for short term gains? Such a course must be advocated against very strongly.

**Remedial Measures**

Concerted efforts are required to resolve Assam ailments. Development and improvement of the economic climate and the situation of the people at large –these are the issues that are agitating the population.

Should the talks with ULFA take off and a ceasefire be contemplated, we must learn lessons from our mistakes with handling the NSCN (I&M), DHD, Karbis and others – the ULFA must be brought into camps on Indian soil and made to give up their weapons –they must not be permitted fresh recruitment, reorganisation, refitting, rearming, extortion or be allowed to take control of the state as was done in the '80s or in the case of the NSCN (I&M). They must not under any circumstances be permitted to interfere with the elections. Ceasefire ground rules must be clearly and carefully worked out in consultation with the Army and the police.

It must also be realised that there is a clear division in ULFA ranks –the leadership and their supporters controlled by the ISI/DGFI in Bangladesh and those on the ground who still operate under at least part of the original ULFA ideals. We must deal with the latter and not the former to bring an end to the problem. In the overall and long-term context, we will at some stage in the near future have to negotiate with Pakistan and Bangladesh to find long-term solutions as the proxy war continues.

## Handling the Bodo Problem
This must be handled carefully and the aspirations of all met. The Bodo Accord must be implemented in letter and spirit as promised and a system of consociation politics imposed within the Bodo Council to avoid the minority groups being alienated by the Bodos. The same issues that apply to the ULFA should govern talks with the NDFB that are likely in the near future.

## Policy on South Assam
The situation here again needs to be handled with care, as this is part of the area claimed by NSCN. Consociation politics, grass root autonomy and economic development are imperative to resolve differences between ethnic groups otherwise ethnic strife will continue to surface. All this has to be coupled with a clamp down on NSCN and other insurgent group activities in the area and the area denied to them for sanctuary.

As all insurgent groups transiting to and from Bangladesh are extensively using the area, border guarding by the BSF must be strengthened. The Assam government must also ensure development of the Bengali-speaking belt in Cachar, Hailakundi and Karimganj failing which we could well see this area develop into a yet another fundamentalist hub.

## Bringing About Peace and Ethnic Harmony
In the preceding chapter, I have covered the economic aspects that need to be addressed with a view to ensure economic progress and development. The Assamese majority must realise that though they form the ethnic majority, they form only about 30–40% of the population with the balance being a multitude of other ethnic groups. Assam will not enjoy peace and prosperity unless it looks after these minorities as their own people. This implies ensuring balanced and not vote bank-related development. Similarly, infrastructure and industry that are to be planned for Assam must also be located and set up to cater for the

needs of the entire region. This is particularly so as the hill states have comparatively small populations, whereas industry needs larger demand volumes to be cost effective. This emphasises the need for the North-East Council to become more effective and ensure more balanced development. It must not humour particular states, simply because the dealing staff happens to be from that state, as has been occurring in the past. Private sector and entrepreneurship must be given much greater impetus as the future lies in that realm.

## KEY ISSUES: THE NAGA PROBLEM AND MANIPUR

### Talks with the Nagas to Resolve Problems

The major issue and stumbling block in the talks between the NSCN (I&M) is the issue of Greater Nagaland. Also, Delhi is being perceived by many as partial and making the Tangkhuls, who form the majority of the NSCN (I&M), supreme over the entire area. Since talks have taken place only with NSCN (I&M), it is perceived as talks only with the Tangkhuls (even Issac Swu, a Sema has not been permitted by Muivah to attend any talks involving policy matters). This will probably not in the long run be accepted by the other tribes, who are deeply distrustful of the Tangkhuls; and in event of an accord with them by the centre may not result in lasting peace. Delhi's approach therefore is fraught with danger.

### Constraints of the Centre

Delhi cannot obviously agree to create Greater Nagaland, as it would have similar demands from all other ethnic groups and result in major disturbances and agitation all over the north-east. It cannot also give power to the NSCN (I&M) in Nagaland, as this will amount to Nagaland being ruled by non-Nagaland tribes led by the Tangkhuls. It can again not agree to a very high degree of autonomy, as that would have repercussions on the federal structure of the entire Indian Union in general and the north-east in particular. There would be little point in getting involved in a blame game for the mess we have created. The question now is how to find a way ahead.

### Remedial Options

I must reiterate that one cannot look at resolution of the Naga problem in isolation, as it is intricately linked to Assam, Manipur, Arunachal

Pradesh, Mizoram and Myanmar in particular and the rest of the north-east in general, including Bangladesh. The errors that have been made till date are in trying to find a solution for Nagaland and not for the region in its totality. Consequent to political boundaries having been created arbitrarily, with various ethnic groups being split across the same and these boundaries now becoming a highly emotive issue for all states in the region; Delhi will need to sell the idea to all those involved, that these boundaries are purely for administration and not related to the concept of territorial integrity of nation states. This will not be so easy, as the people of the region are still heaped in their primordial value system, wherein territorial integrity of the nation remains a core value; and it would be quite sometime before they transit to modernity in all its facets.

The answers therefore perhaps lie in the realm of transiting to modernity more rapidly; wherein integration, consociation politics, economic development and culture need to be given greater importance than aspects of territorial integrity and sovereignty, for all ethnic groups as a whole. Whilst doing so it should be ensured that no favouritism is shown to a single ethnic group simply because they are agitating, as this would only result in other ethnic groups rebelling against the state. This is particularly so as there has been traditionally deep-rooted distrust between the different ethnic groups, including amongst the Nagas.

## Broaden Base for Talks
In my view, Delhi needs to first, broaden its base for dialogue, involving various ethnic groups, all the major dissenting factions, the church, intellectuals who understand the region, and representatives of all governments involved and NOT simply the NSCN (I&M).

## Impose Presidents Rule and enforce Proper Administration, Development
President's Rule needs to be imposed in Nagaland, Manipur and areas affected by the problem in Assam and Arunachal for some time, with approval of Parliament, so as to be able to directly administer these regions, resolve problems and ensure rapid economic progress and development. To this end, governors need to be carefully selected, given a free hand and if there is a need to replace existing administrators, this should be done. All development needs to be in accordance with the will of the local people.

### Restore Rule of Law

The rule of law in all areas needs to be restored by a crackdown on all insurgent groups including the NSCN groups who are equally culpable for the existing state of affairs. This would mean induction of additional security forces, which should be accepted, and they need to be given a free hand with strict instructions to conduct people friendly operations with minimum possible infringements on human rights. If this means a breakdown of the ceasefire, this should be accepted. The judiciary needs to be re-activated. The police force needs to be revitalised through reorganisation, training and modernised and progressively made effective so as to take charge of policing the state properly. Politicians continuing to play up to the insurgents should be sternly dealt with. Unfortunately it appears that the Government is bending over backwards to meet even arbitrary demands of the NSCN (I &M) as is evinced from Muivah's recent statements and demands and the Government's reactions to the same as reported in the media.

### Curb the Black Insurgent Economy and Revitalise the Police

Extortion, drug and arms smuggling by all insurgent groups across the board should be reined in, including the NSCN (I&M) and (K), and their intimidation of the local population stopped. Both the NSCN factions need to be made to abide by the terms of the ceasefire if necessary by force, even if this means a breakdown of the ceasefire. In case this happens, security forces need to be given a free hand to deal with the situation, but at the same time ensure people friendly operations with minimum possible violation of human rights. A foreign policy offensive needs to be launched to deny external support to the insurgents. All this needs to be done by explaining the reasons for doing so publicly to the people.

### Put a Stop to Extortion

Extortion, intimidation and crime need to be brought under control. The security forces must take all possible measures to prevent and stop inter ethnic strife and bloodshed and wherever this occurs, ringleaders must be brought to justice.

### Restore Normalcy

These are only the initial measures which need to be taken immediately to send a clear message to the entire population that we mean business and that all possible measures will be taken to restore normalcy to the states and that all ethnic groups and their problems would be handled impartially and promptly.

**Concerted Efforts towards Economic Development**
With ethnic emotions running high, there is no option but to bring this under control through a concerted developmental and economic effort with an abundance of funds and employment generation in a balanced manner in all ethnic areas simultaneously. All such development work needs to be in accordance with the will of the local people. Private enterprise and self-employment schemes should be given impetus and private investment would be encouraged the moment the law and order situation is brought under control. SM families and ESM should be brought to the forefront in the economic and developmental effort in light of the very high numbers that there are in the state. Government control over all border trade should be immediately established along with a free trade zone on the Myanmar border to facilitate trade and revenue accrual to the government. It needs to be realised that the Moreh border offers the best possible access route for trade not only with Myanmar but also the South-East Asian region. This needs to be developed on priority and capitalised upon. Manipur must get all weather road access to all neighbouring states, particularly Assam so that the Meiteis are not intimidated by all and sundry. Manipur is rich in natural resources – trade with its neighbours must be encouraged. The rail link to Manipur and if possible its extension up to the Myanmar border needs to be pushed through on the highest priority. All possible interaction and measures should be instituted to counter the feeling of alienation that has crept in to all ethnic groups alike and to win them over through all possible measures including economic activity and development.

**Forming a Panel**
The widened talks suggested to attempt to resolve the Naga problem, by a 'panel' who know and understand the region, should also encompass representatives of the ethnic groups of Manipur. A major fall-out of the Naga problem is an increasing deterioration in the situation in Manipur. The same 'Panel' needs to also be given the responsibilities of making recommendations and method to be adopted for Manipur's malaise. To my mind, however with the problems being what they are,

I can see no option but to create an economic and developmental federation of ethnic regions, with political boundaries being purely for the purposes of administration, coupled with consociation politics. Cultural and social trans-state linkages on ethnic issues can then be worked out and interwoven into the above structure to obviate the demands for greater Nagaland and Mizoram. Inter-ethnic seminars and discussions involving maximum people should be undertaken to remove the causes for ethnic strife.

All the above cannot be accomplished in a day. The first requirement is to re-establish the rule of law, coupled with good administration, followed then by all other activities. It must be understood that, w ith such complicated problems and the situation being what it is, problem resolution in this troubled state will be a time consuming and complex affair.

**Key Issues: Mizoram**

Mizoram, though a relatively peaceful state needs to resolve its problems with its minorities through consociation politics and economic development. If this is not done, agitation and strife at some stage is inevitable, as there is a perception that its minorities are being neglected.

It should try to avoid involvement in the problems of the Kuki–Chin tribals of Manipur and Chin hills (demographically the same stock) and issues of Greater Mizoram, as this only complicates the problem resolution of these issues.

It also needs to resolve issues of disorganised development, which have resulted in neglect of the agricultural sector and consequently very large-scale migration towards urbanisation (58% or more of the population is now urban), which is simply not sustainable. Today the towns are literally bursting at the seams with the infrastructure being unable to support such an influx—the terrain and soil structure are also unable to support the very high population densities that now exist in the towns. With most of Mizoram being in a high seismic zone with very high rainfall patterns, the urban areas are literally time bombs, God forbid, should a natural calamity occur on the lines of the recent earthquake in Pakistan and Kashmir!

It is also very highly dependent for its survival on central assistance, with jobs being available primarily only in the government sector. It has a major drug abuse problem and a high incidence of HIV. Its major problems today are in the social, economic and developmental spheres. These need to be attended to on the highest priority on the lines suggested in the preceding chapter on economy and development, to avoid social and economic hardship and strife.

## Key Issues: Arunachal

Arunachal is fortunate in having a small population spread over a huge area thereby reducing to a degree the possibility of ethnic strife. Notwithstanding this fact, there is a fair amount of distrust and rivalry between its multitudes of ethnic groups, the majority of whom strongly feel that the 'Adi' majority is neglecting them. It is for this reason and the fact that the NSCN also claim Tirap, Changlang and parts of Lohit district, that it is embroiled in a low-grade insurgency. The only way in which such problems can be resolved is through consociation politics and economic development, with much more attention paid by the majority ethnic group to the minorities. The state also has a migrant problem, which needs to be addressed considering its small population size. Arunachal is again heavily dependent on Delhi for doles even though it has tremendous availability of natural resources. This needs to be progressively reduced and the state's efforts diverted towards drawing in investment, private entrepreneurship and self-employment schemes. Delhi and the NEC need to concentrate on greater efforts towards development of infrastructure, as it is woefully inadequate.

## Key Issues: Meghalaya

Meghalaya needs to attend to its migrant problem as suggested for Assam and consequently keep its low-grade insurgency under control, particularly in the Garo Hills where the ULFA, NDFB and the ANVC have sanctuary/are active. Though the police are doing a fair job, they need modernisation and training to deal with the problems adequately particularly since the state is a major transit route for migrants and insurgents to and from Bangladesh. Here again, the problem of Bangladesh support and sanctuary to the insurgents need urgent attention. The Khasis and Garos need to come to terms with each other and live amicably –again consociation politics is the need of the day. Recent events like the killing of Garo students by the police can only add to the alienation the Garos now feel. Though the state has tremendous economic potential, it is financially backward. A concerted effort must be made towards economic development, employment generation in the private sector and reduced dependence on doles.

## Key Issues: Tripura

Tripura's majority Bengali population must look after its tribal minority and give them a fair deal, all the more so since it is the migrants who today form the majority and are therefore the source of the problem. A rational social, cultural, economic and developmental package must be worked out and given to them and consociation politics brought to the fore. The ultimate solution would only be possible through linking hands in economic development and getting Bangladesh to desist from supporting the insurgents.

## Key Issues: Sikkim

Sikkim is till date doing a commendable job in looking after its minorities –it should continue to do so through greater economic development and tourism. It needs to however take conscious note of the developments in Nepal and ensure that west Sikkim does not provide sanctuary to Maoists and Islamic fundamentalists, or get involved in the issue of Gurkhaland. A few media reports of recent times indicate that there are attempts to do so. To this end, it needs to modernise and train its police force to handle such a situation and prevent this from happening.

## Key Issues: North Bengal

Notwithstanding objections to considering North Bengal part of the north-east, I would reiterate that from the point of view of geography, history, demography and sociology, this area besides being the gateway to the region, is very much part of the north-east. It also needs to be noted that the demography and problems of people in the Siliguri Corridor are very similar to that of lower Assam; and that of the hill district of Darjeeling being similar to Sikkim. The Siliguri corridor has problems of the KLO, separatism in Cooch Behar due to lack of socio economic attention, Bhutanese dissidents, being a sanctuary for the ULFA, NDFB, Maoists, Islamic fundamentalists, large scale migration, social problems of the tea tribes from the ailing tea industry, and a percolation of Bihar's law and order problems, with the associated hassles of social deprivation, poverty and neglect of the minorities. While some efforts are being made by the government to deal with the problem, a much more concerted effort is needed to handle the problems at hand. Consociation politics are imperative to handle these problems, coupled with greater efforts towards economic development in this area. To this end, it would be well worth the governments' while to have this suggestion examined in detail by a suitably composed panel.

It also needs noting that Siliguri is the gateway and supply base to the north-east and also for trade with China through Sikkim when it takes off. Siliguri needs to be properly developed as an industrial and trading base –this would generate employment and greater prosperity and ease the problems of the area. With the problems that there are, much greater effort needs to be put in to modernise and train the police to handle the situation –it is still nowhere near what is required. Darjeeling, Jalpaiguri and Cooch Behar districts needs to be handled, with tact, diplomacy and care –there is still a great deal of feeling of neglect amongst the population. Again consociation politics are required. There are also rumours and media reports of Maoists taking sanctuary in the area. If true, the situation needs to be urgently nipped in the bud. Much greater economic and developmental efforts are required particularly in the fields of tourism, rejuvenation of the tea industry, drawing in investment, private entrepreneurship, self-employment and attention to welfare and employment of the large number of ex-servicemen of the district.

## Conclusion

I must reiterate in conclusion that the problems of the north-east region though extremely complex, can be resolved through dialogue with the people of the region and by collectively applying our minds to find the best possible solution for the population at large. I would be more than satisfied if the views offered in this book even partially contribute to the endeavours by those in authority towards problem resolution. In my view, we owe the wonderful people of the north-east a wholehearted and sincere effort towards resolution of their problems.

# LIST OF ABBREVIATIONS

| | |
|---|---|
| ANVC | Achik National Volunteer Force |
| ABSU | All Bodo Students Union |
| AASU | All Assam Students Union |
| AGP | Assam Gana Parishad |
| AAGSP | All Assam Gana Sangram Parishad |
| ATTF | All Tripura Tiger Force |
| AFSPA | Armed Forces Special Powers Act |
| AMULFA | All Muslim United Liberation Forum of Assam |
| Bodo SF | Bodo Security Force |
| BAC | Bodo Autonomous Council |
| BLT | Bodo Liberation Tigers |
| BNLF | Bru National Liberation Force |
| CNA | Chin National Army |
| CI | Counter Insurgency |
| CPO | Central Police Organisations |
| DHD | Dima Halim Daoga |
| DGFI | Director General Forces Intelligence (Bangladesh) |
| ESM | Ex-servicemen |
| ISI | Inter Services Intelligence (Pakistan) |
| IMDT | Illegal Immigrants Determination Tribunal |
| J & K | Jammu and Kashmir |
| GNLF | Gurkha National Liberation Front |
| HUJI | Harkat-ul-Jehad-al-Islami |
| HNLC | Hynniewtrep National Liberation Council |
| HPC | Hmar peoples Convention |
| KLO | Kamtapur Liberation Organisation |
| KNA | Kuki National Army |
| KLA | Kuki Liberation Army |
| KNF | Kuki National Front |
| KYKL | Kanglei Yawol Kungla Lup |
| LC | Line of Control |

# LIST OF ABBREVIATIONS

| | |
|---|---|
| LAC | Line of Actual Control |
| LTTE | Liberation Tigers of Tamil Eelam |
| MNF | Mizo National Front |
| Maoist | Communist Party (Marxist – Leninist – Maoist) |
| MISA | Maintenance of Internal Security Act |
| MULTA | Muslim United Liberation Tigers of Assam |
| MPA | Manipur Peoples Army |
| NSCN (I&M) | National Socialist Council of Nagalim (Muivah and Issaac Swu) |
| NSCN (K) | National Socialist Council of Nagalim (KhaplÒang) |
| NNC | Naga National Council |
| NFG | Naga Federal Government |
| NDFB | National Democratic Front of Bodoland |
| NEFA | North East Frontier Agency |
| NLFT | National Liberation Front of Tripura |
| NLFA | National Liberation Front of Arunachal |
| PLA | Peoples' Liberation Army |
| PMF | Para Military Organisations |
| POTA | Prevention of Terrorism Act |
| POCA | Prevention of Organised Crime Act |
| PREPAK | Peoples Revolutionary Party of Kangleipak |
| RPF | Revolutionary Peoples' Front |
| SF | Security Forces |
| SULFA | Surrendered ULFA cadres |
| SM | Servicemen |
| TADA | Terrorist and Disruptive Activities Prevention Act |
| ULFA | United Liberation Front of Assam |
| UNLF | United National Liberation Front |
| UPVA | United Peoples Volunteers of Arunachal Pradesh |
| ZRA | Zomi Revolutionary Army |

# SELECTED BIBLIOGRAPHY

'Aakrosh', *Asian Journal of Terrorism and International Conflicts*, Forum for Strategic and Security Studies.
Aizawl Official Records
All Central and State Government websites on the north-east and its states.
'Anxiety and Anger in India's North East', paper presented at Centre for Conflict Development in India's North-east, Guwahati.
———, 'Multi-Force Operations in Counter Terrorism: a View from the Assam Theatre', paper presented at Centre for Conflict Development in India's North-east, Guwahati.
———, 'Naga Identity, Meitei Nationalism and Electoral Politics', paper presented at Centre for Conflict Development in India's Northeast, Guwahati.
———, 'Peace in Naga Country', paper presented at Centre for Conflict Development in India's North-east, Guwahati.
Ao L, *Rural Development in Nagaland*.
Ao Tajenyuba, *The British Occupation of Naga Country*.
Archives, *Assam Tribune*.
———, *North East Times*.
———, *Sentinel*.
———, *North East Daily*.
———, *Nagaland Post*.
———, Articles on 'Islamic Fundamentalism in Pakistan and Bangladesh', *Herald*, Pakistan.
———, *Shillong Times*.
———, *Arunachal Post*.
———, *Imphal Daily*.
———, *Mizoram Times*.
———, *Statesman*, Calcutta.
Ashley J Tellis, Article in 'Carnegie Endowment for International Peace', *United States and South Asia*.
Aziz K K, *Murder of History in Pakistan*.
Bareh H M, *Encyclopedia of North East India*, 2001.
Barry Buzan, *People States and Fear: the National Security Problem in International Relations*.
Baruah S L, *Comprehensive History of Assam*.
Baruah Sanjib, *India Against Itself: Assam and the Politics of Nationality*.
Basak R G, *History of North Eastern India*.
Bauah Dr (Mrs) S L, *A Comprehensive History of Assam*.

# SELECTED BIBLIOGRAPHY

Bell Sir Charles, *Tibet: Past and Present*, Clarendon Press, Oxford, 1924.
Bell, *Past and Present*, Tibet.
Bhasin A S, *Nepal's Relation's with India and China*.
Bhat S C, *The Triangle: India-Nepal-China, a Study of Treaty Relations*.
Bhatkoti U D, *Sino Pakistan Relations: A Chinese Perspective*.
Bhattacharjea S R, *Tribal Insurgency in Tripura*.
Bhaumik Subir, *Insurgent Cross Fire – North East India*
Bhawan Raj Records, Shillong
Bhola P L, *Pakistan-China Relations*.
Bhutto Zulfikar Ali, *Myth of Independence*
Bindra, *Indo-Bangladesh Relations*.
British official records and reports of Bengal and Assam, National Library, Kolkata.
Bunji Ahom, *A Chronicle of Assam in Tai-Ahom*, Golap Chandra Baruah (trans.).
Census of India, Government of India, 1991, 2001.
Chabra K M L, *Assam Challenge*.
Chaherbhuj, *Tribes of North East India*.
Chandra Bhuyan, *History of Assam*.
Chatterjee Partha, *The State and Politics in India*.
Christof Von Furer Haimendorf, *Return to the Naked Nagas*.
Clark Mary Mead, *A Corner in India*, American Baptist Church (pub.).
Coelho V H, *Sikkim and Bhutan*.
Constantine R, *Manipur: Maid of the Mountains*.
Dai Mamang, *Arunachal Pradesh: the Myth of Tranquility*.
Daniel L Byman and Roger Cliff, *China's Arms Sales: Motivations and Implications*, Rand, 1999.
Das Gurudas, 'Probable Options – Cementing the Faultlines in Assam', Northeast State Papers.
___, *Migration, Ethnicity and Competition for State Resources: Explanation of the Social Tension in North East India*.
Das H N, 'Insurgency and Development: the Assam Experience', revised version of author's paper presented at seminar on 'Addressing Conflicts In India's North East' Institute for Conflict Management, June 25–27, 2001, New Delhi.
Das N K, *Ethnic Identity, Ethnicity and Social Stratification in North East India*.
Das Samir Kumar, *Ethnic Conflict and Internal Security – A Plea for Reconstructing Civil Society in Assam*.
___, 'Assam Insurgency and Disintegration of Civil Society', earlier draft paper presented at seminar on 'National Security Issues: Special Emphasis on Northeastern India', Omeo Kumar Das Institute of Social Change and Development, Guwahati, April 22–24, 2002.
Das Samir Kumar, *ULFA – A Political Analysis*.
___, *Foreign Hand in Theory*.
Deb Bimal J, *Development Priorities in North East India*.
Devi L, *Ahom Tribal Relations*.
Downs F S, *Christianity in North East India: Historical Perspective*.
Dutt V P, *India's Foreign Policy in a Changing World*.
Elwin Verrier, *A Philosophy For NEFA*.

# SELECTED BIBLIOGRAPHY

'Extremist Islamic Consolidation', *Faultlines*, Vol. 14, Bangladesh, July 2003.
*Faultlines:* Writings on Conflict and Resolution, Institute of Conflict Management, New Delhi.
Gate Edward, *A History of Assam.*
Gate, E A *Gazeteer of Bengal and North East India.*
___, *A History of Assam.*
Ghosh S K, *India's North East Frontier.*
Gill K P S, *The Imperatives of National Security Legislation in India*, New Delhi, April 2002.
Gopalakrishnan R, *The North East India: Land, Economy and People.*
Gori Gulab Khan, *The Changing Phase of Tribal Areas of Manipur.*
Hazarika Sanjay, *Strangers in the Mist.*
Horam M, *Thirty Years of Naga Insurgency.*
Hrishikeshan K, 'Assam's Agony', based on paper presented at seminar on 'Hurdles to Resolving Conflict in Assam', Institute for Conflict Management, Project on 'Planning for Security & Development', May 1, 2002.
Hussain Monirul, *The Assam Movement: Class, Ideology and Identity.*
Hussain Wasbir, 'Cross Border Human Traffic in South Asia: Demographic Inversion,
Hussain, *The Assam Movement.*
Imchon Panger, *Ancient Ao Religion and Culture.*
Imti Alba, *Reminiscence: Impur to NNC.*
Institute of Peace and Conflict Studies website.
Internet Sites of All North Eastern Insurgent Groups.
Jacob Lt Gen J F R, *Surrender at Dacca: Birth of a Nation.*
Jaffa V S, *Ten O'Clock to Bed.*
___, 'Insouciance in the Face of Terror', *Faultlines: Writings on Conflict and*
John Herz, *The Nation State and the Crisis of World Politics.*
John Vanlalhnuna, *Church and Political Upheaval in Mizoram.*
John W Garver, *The Chinese–India–US Triangle.*
Johnstone Sir James, *My Experiences in Naga Hills and Manipur.*
Kadian Rajesh, *Tibet, India and China.*
Kanchan L, 'Negotiating Insurgencies: the Naga Imbroglio', *Faultlines: Writings on Conflict & Resolution.*
Karim Maj Gen Afsir, *Kashmir: the Troubled Frontier.*
Kumar Anand, *Renewed Thrust of ISI and Al Qaeda in North East.*
___, *A New Destination for Radical Islamists.*
___, *The ULFA Business in Bangladesh.*
Lalmachuana, *Some Aspects of Mizoram Economy and Development.*
Lanusong T, *Nagaland: A Study in Social Geography.*
Lesser O Ian, 'Countering the New Terrorism', *Rand Report.*
Lintner B, *Land of Jade* (Banned by NSCN).
Malhotra V P, *Defence Related Treaties of India.*
Mallik S K, *Quranic Concept of War.*
Mark Burles and Abram N Shulsky, *Patterns in China's Use of Force: Evidence from History and Doctrinal Writings*, Rand.

Marwah Ved, *Uncivil Wars: Pathology of Terrorism.*
―――, *India's Security Challenges.*
Mazumdar R C, *History of Bengal.*
Mishra Udayan, *The Periphery Strikes Back.*
Nag Sajal, 'Withdrawal Syndrome: Secessionism in Modern North East India', *Essays on North-East India*, Indus, New Delhi, 1994.
Nandy Ashish, *The Political Culture of the Indian State.*
Narahari N S, *Security Threats to North East India.*
―――, *Socio Ethnic Conflicts in the North East.*
Nath Sunil, 'The Secessionist Insurgency and Freedom of Minds', North East State papers.
Nayyar A H, Ahmad Salim, *The Subtle Subversion: the State of Curricula and Textbooks in Pakistan.*
Nepram Binalakshmi, *South Asia's Fractured Frontier: Armed Conflict, Narcotics and*
Nirmal Nibedon, *The Dagger Brigade.*
Norbu Dawa, *Tibet: The Road Ahead.*
Pemberton P V, 'Report on the Eastern Frontier of India', DHAS
Pillai K R, *India's Foreign Policy in the 1990s.*
Pillai Lt Gen S K, *Anatomy of an Insurgency; Ethnicity and Identity in Nagaland.*
'Points of View', Department of Public Relations, Government of Assam.
Prasad R N, *Government and Politics in Mizoram.*
Quraishi Humra, *The Forgotten State.*
Rahman Sheikh Mujibur, *East Pakistan: its Population and Economics.*
Ram Rahul, *Modern Bhutan.*
Raman B, Articles on issues of Jehadi Terrorism and associated subjects, Institute of Topical Studies, Chennai.
Raman B, *Maoists Gain Momentum in India.*
Ramana P V, *Networking Conspiracy in the North East: Partners in Crime.*
Rammohan E N, *Manipur – A Degenerated Insurgency.*
Ramunny, *The World of Nagas.*
Rao General K V Krishna, *Prepare or Perish.*
*Resolution*, Vol. 5, May 2000.
―――, 'Counterinsurgency Warfare; the Use and Abuse of Military Force', *Faultlines: Writings on Conflict and Resolution*, Vol. 3, November 1999.
Richardson H E, *Tibet and Its History*, Oxford University Press, Toronto, 1962.
Risely H H, *The Gazeteer of Sikkim.*
Robert H Donaldson, *Soviet Policy Towards India: Ideology and Strategy.*
Routray Bibhu Prasad, *ULFA: the Revolution Comes a Full Circle.*
Sachdeva Gulshan, *Economy of the North East: Policy, Present Conditions and Future Prospects.*
Sahni Ajai, 'Terror by Another Name', *Faultlines: Writings on Conflict and Resolution*,
Saikia Jaideep, 'ISI Reaches East', *Faultlines*, Vol. 6, New Delhi, 2000.
―――, *Terror Sans Frontiers: Islamic Militancy in North East India.*
―――, *Development Challenges in India: Assam in 2015.*
―――, 'Revolutionaries or Warlords: ULFA's Organisational Profile', *Faultlines: Writings on Conflict and Resolution*, Vol. 9, New Delhi, July 2001.

# SELECTED BIBLIOGRAPHY

___, *Allies in the Closet: Overground Linkages and Terrorism in Assam.*
___, 'Autumn in Springtime: the ULFA Battles for Survival, *Faultlines: Writings on Conflict and Resolution*, Vol. 7, New Delhi, November 2000.
Sandhya Goswami, *Language Politics in Assam.*
Sanjayya, *Assam – A Crisis of Identity.*
Sanjemnbam Vedaja, *Manipur: Geography and Regional Development*
Sanyu Visier, *What Nagaland State Did to the Nagas: a Historical Perspective.*
___, *A History of the Nagas and Nagaland.*
___, *The Noxious Web: Insurgency in the North East.*
Sardesai S C, *The Patkoi Nagas.*
Sareen Sushant, *The Jihad Factory: Pakistan's Islamic Revolution in the Making*
Sarkar J N, *History of Bengal.*
Sengupta Dipankar, *Insurgency in North East India: the Role of Bangladesh.*
Shashinungla, *Insurgency and Factional Intransigence.*
___, *Nagaland: the Dynamics of Extortion.*
Shouri Arun, *Will the Iron Fence Save a Tree Hollowed by Termites.*
Singh Jasjit Air Cmdr, *Nuclear India*, Knowledge World, New Delhi, 1998. Appadorai, *Selected Documents on India's Foreign Policy.*
Singh B P, *A Problem of Change: a Study of North East India.*
Singh Jasjit, *Nuclear India.*
Singh K S, *People of India.*
Singh Prakash, *Nagaland.*
Singh W Ibohal, *History of Manipur.*
Sinha Lt Gen S K, 'Illegal Immigration into Assam', Report available at http://www.satp.org/India/Documents/Assam.
Sinha S K, *Violence and Hope in India's North East.*
*Small Arms Proliferation in India's North East.*
South Asia Terrorism Portal. www.satp.org
Sree Venkataraman, *Our People Our World: a Fight for Tribal Identity.*
Swaine Michael D and Ashley J Tellis, *Interpreting China's Grand Strategy: Past, Present and Future*, Rand.
The Wiles of War: 36 Military Strategies from Ancient China
Thompson Robert, *Defeating Communist Insurgency*, Chatto and Windus, London, 1966.
'ULFA's links with Bangladesh', *The Hindu*, September 8, 1992.
Upadhyaya R, *ULFA: A Deviated Movement.*
Verghese B G, *India's North East Resurgent – Ethnicity, Insurgency and Governance.* Vol. 9, New Delhi, July 2001.
___, *Security and Development in India's North-East.*
___, *Anti POTA Hysteria.*
___, 'Terrorist Economy in India's North East – Preliminary Explorations', *Faultlines: Writings on Conflict & Resolution*, Vol. 8, ICM-Bulwark Books, New Delhi, April 2001.
Wikipedia, *Free Encyclopedia: History of North East India*
Wilkinson Paul, *Terrorism versus Democracy.*

# INDEX

Achik National Volunteer Council   47
Adis   6, 55, 59
AFSPA   107, 110–16
Ahoms   7–9, 11, 19, 28, 41, 57
All Assam Students Union   19
All Bodo Students Union   23
Apatani   55
Armed Forces Special Powers Act   45, 107, 110
Aryans   5, 6
Arunachal Pradesh   3, 5–7, 10–11, 13–15, 17, 27, 30, 33–4, 36, 43, 44, 55–9, 67, 74, 78, 91, 93, 101, 105, 111, 122–3, 127
Army not to perform police functions   109
Nagaland   3, 5–13, 15, 17–25, 27, 30–4, 36, 39–41, 43–5, 47–50, 52–3, 55–9, 62, 65, 67, 68, 70, 75, 78, 81–2, 89–90, 96, 101,105, 109, 111, 117–23, 125, 127, 128
Assam Gana Parishad   20, 120
Assam Rifles   56–7, 65, 70, 109, 111
Assam – problems   25
Assam Accord   20, 24, 78
Austrics   5–6, 52, 60–1

Balkanisation of Assam a mistake   93
Bangladeshi migrations   24, 31, 48–9, 56, 58, 61,
Bangladesh strategy for proxy war   77
Bangladeshi Lebensraum   21–2, 89,
Birth of ULFA   19–21
Birth of NSCN   33–4
Bodo movement, Bodo Accord, Bodo Autonomous Region   23–4, 121

Bodo Security Force, Bodo Autonomous Council,   23
Border Peace and Tranquillity Accord   58, 79
British   9–15, 17, 27–31, 39, 41, 43, 47, 49–50, 53, 56–7, 60, 62, 73, 94
British instigated migrations   10, 41
Bringing about ethnic peace and harmony   121–2
Bhutan   3, 6–8, 11, 22–3, 55, 59–61, 74, 82–3, 90, 119, 128
Bhutan operations   22–3
Bhutias 59–61
Bhutto – *The Myth of Independence*   21
Burmese   47, 56, 76

Causes of Naga discontent   35
Causes of Manipur Problem   37
Causes of Antagonism of Bangladesh and Pakistan   74
Cease Fire   23–4, 34–5, 44–6, 79, 109, 118–20, 124
Chandel   40–1, 66
Chakmas   51–3, 56, 58, 93
Chittagong Hill Tracts   42, 53
Churachandpur   40–1
Cold war   14, 75, 77
Consociation politics   94, 121, 123, 126–9
Counterinsurgency operations   43, 52, 76, 109
Crown Colony   31
Cr PC 130–1   108
Curbing Politician, insurgent, businessman nexus   102

# INDEX

Dealing with migration  118
Demands of NSCN  36
Demands of people of Nagaland  36
Demography of
   Assam  17
   Nagaland  27
   Manipur  39
   Arunachal  55
   Tripura  52
   Meghalaya  47
   Mizoram  49
   Sikkim  59
   North Bengal  61
   Meghalaya  38
   Ex-servicemen  65
Director General Force Intelligence Bangladesh  24, 118–19, 120
Disturbed Areas  112
Dravidians  5

Economic Issues  54
Effects of Partition  13, 73
Effects of Migration  11
Effects of China falling out with USSR  75
Effects if government accedes to NSCN demands  36
Effects of Indo-China dispute  57–8, 59
Effect of Pakistani defeat  76
Effects of 9/11  81
Effects attack on Indian Parliament  81
Effects US operations in Iraq  82
Ethnic strife in South Assam  24–5
Ex-servicemen's welfare – remedial measures necessary  68–71

Foreign Trade  103

Garo  6, 27, 47–9, 52, 93, 127
Greater Mizoram  40, 43–4, 50–1, 126
Greater Nagaland  25, 34–6, 40, 44, 46, 59, 122, 126

Handling the Bodo problem  121
Higher technical education  103
Hmars, Paites  40, 51, 93
Human Rights and the Security Forces  115
Hyniewtrep National Liberation Council  48

Illegal Migrants Determination Act  24, 72, 89
Importance of political resolution  106
Indo -China Border Dispute  57–8
Inner Line  10–1, 29, 31, 50, 57, 94, 103
Instigated Migration  10
Inter Services Intelligence Pakistan  20–1, 24, 118–20
Inter Ethnic Conflict in Manipur  40

Jamatias  52

Kamtapuri  6, 11–12, 61–2
Kamrupa  6, 7, 61
Karbis  5, 23, 25, 47, 94, 120
Kargil conflict  79
Khampti, Phakial, Aitonia, Turung, Tai Shan  18
Khasi – Jaintia  5, 47, 48
Koch  6, 24, 61
Konyak  27, 57
Kuki – Chin – Mizos- Zoumis - Zou  7, 10, 13, 30, 39–47, 49, 51–2, 66, 126

Labour policy  103
Lalung, Chutiya  6–7
Lepcha  5, 6, 12, 59, 60

Macmohan Line  57
Manipur  3, 6–7, 9–10, 13–14, 17, 27, 30, 33–7, 39–46, 49–52, 65–6, 76, 78, 81–2, 96, 101, 105, 109, 111, 114, 119, 122–3, 125–6
Maoist activity  61–3, 75, 82–3, 90, 128–9

# INDEX

Meghalaya  3, 5–6, 12, 15, 47–9, 51, 53, 67, 78, 81, 105, 111, 127
Meitei  6, 13–15, 39–46, 66, 109, 125
Meitei Kuki Conflict  43–4
Meitei Naga Conflict  14, 39, 40, 42–4, 45, 109
Method of Army operation in counterinsurgency  109
Mishmi  6, 55–6
Miri  55
Mizoram  3, 7, 14, 39–40, 42–7, 49–54, 66–7, 76, 78, 96, 100, 106, 111, 123, 126
Mizo National Front  50–1
Mizo Accord  51, 96
Mizoram model  96
Moamaria Insurgency  8–9
Marans and Muttocks  8–9
Mongoloid Migrations  5–7
Monpa  55–6
Muslims  6, 11, 17–19, 39, 53, 73–4, 83, 120
Mughals  8, 18, 28, 41, 62
Myanmar invasions  41, 47

Nagaland  3, 14, 17, 25, 27–37, 39–40, 42–7, 50, 55, 57–9, 66, 69, 78, 96, 101, 105, 109, 111, 119, 122, 123, 126
Naga Tribes  6, 29–31, 34–6, 39, 40–1, 44, 46, 56
Nagas –identity and ethnicity  29, 30
Naga Club  30–1
Naga National Council  31
Naga Plebiscite  32
Nagalim  20, 25, 30, 33, 36, 81
Naga Language  19
Naga Federal Government  32–3, 40, 43
Naga Tribes in Manipur  39–41, 44
Naga Kuki Strife  43
National Security – duties of the state  87
National Socialist Council of Nagalim  20, 25, 30, 33–7, 40, 43–4, 46, 48, 51, 56, 59, 61, 65–6, 78–9, 81, 91, 93, 96, 101, 105, 109, 117–24, 127
National Democratic Front of Bodoland  12, 23–4, 48, 61, 78, 79, 82, 93, 121, 127, 128
Nepal  3, 5, 10–1, 59–61, 63, 82–3, 90, 103, 128
Nepalese  10–2, 18, 47–8, 56, 58–9, 60–2, 82
Negritos  5
Necessity for good governance and dialogue  95–6
Necessity to root out black economy  100–1, 118
Need to focus on agricultural sector  51, 102–3, 126
Nine Point agreement  32
Nishi, Dafla  55
North Bengal  3, 5–6, 12–13, 15, 17, 55, 57, 59–63, 67, 75, 82, 96, 100, 105–6, 128
Nocte  55–6
North East Frontier Agency  14, 33, 57

Options open to resolve Naga problem  122, 125

Pakistan's role in proxy war  77–8, 81, 118, 121
Pakistan's new game plan  82
Phizo  29–30, 32
Policy for South Assam  121
Police must handle insurgency  96, 107
Political awakening  13, 15, 29, 31, 41, 48, 50, 60
Political Structure Nagaland  27
Pragjyotishpura  6
President's rule  20, 123
Prevention of Terrorism Act  114–15
Principles of counter insurgency  106, 107
Problem Areas North Bengal  62–3

# INDEX

Problems centrally controlled economic model  99

Rapprochement with West and China  79
Rapid development of Assam essential for region  117
Reasons of economic failure  88, 100
Reverend Michael Scott  32
Religious Denominations Assam  18
Requirement for balanced foreign policy  83
Requirement to review political structure  93
Restore rule of law in Manipur  124
Riangs – Brus  51–2
Role for Servicemen and ex-servicemen  65–71
Role of Armed Forces  108

Saraighat  8
Senapati  40, 66
Shillong Accord  33
Sikkim  3, 5–6, 10–3, 17, 51, 56, 59, 60–1, 67, 75, 100, 128, 129
Situation in Manipur  46, 109, 114, 119, 125
Sheik Mujibur Rehman  15, 21, 77
Sulung  55
Suggested policy towards West, Russia and China  88
Suggested policy towards Pakistan  88–9
Suggested policy towards Bangladesh  89–90
Suggested policy towards Nepal  90

Suggested policy towards Bhutan  90
Suggested policy towards Myanmar  91
Suggested policy towards S E Asia and Middle East  91
Suggested Role for ex-servicemen  65
Start of Insurgency in Nagaland, Manipur, Mizoram  14, 32, 42
Start of the Proxy War -Chinese and Western Role  77
Stoppage of foreign support  106

Tagin  55
Tangsa  55–6
Tamenglong  43, 66
Talks with NSCN  35, 46
Tibetans  6, 11, 56–8, 60
Tea Tribes  18, 24, 61–2, 128
Tilt towards the West  83
Trimming state apparatus and imposing taxation  102
Tribal Values  28
Tripura  3–4, 6–7, 12–13, 15, 17, 47–54, 67, 75, 78, 81–2, 91, 101, 105, 109, 111, 128
Tuensang  33, 57

Udayachal –demand for state of Bodoland  23
Ukhrul  65–6
ULFA
Use of Military force to quell insurgency  106
Use of ex-servicemen for development  69–71, 96, 125

Wangchoo  55–6